Steven N. Gold
Jan Faust
Editors

Trauma Practice in the Wake of September 11, 2001

Trauma Practice in the Wake of September 11, 2001 has been co-published simultaneously as *Journal of Trauma Practice,* Volume 1, Numbers 3/4 2002.

Pre-publication REVIEWS, COMMENTARIES, EVALUATIONS . . .

"EXTRAORDINARILY TIMELY AND IMPORTANT. . . . It is now a different world that confronts mental health professionals. This book presents both broad theoretical perspectives and the personal accounts of some who have required care and those who provide it. It begins to help us understand the changes of the post 9/11 era–how domestic terrorism has affected the national psyche as well as individuals, inflicting new wounds and awakening old hurts."

James A. Chu, MD
Director
Trauma and Dissociative Disorders Program
McLean Hospital
Belmont
Massachusetts
Editor
Journal of Trauma & Dissociation

Trauma Practice in the Wake of September 11, 2001

Trauma Practice in the Wake of September 11, 2001 has been co-published simultaneously as *Journal of Trauma Practice,* Volume 1, Numbers 3/4 2002.

The *Journal of Trauma Practice*™ Monographic "Separates"

Below is a list of " separates," which in serials librarianship means a special issue simultaneously published as a special journal issue or double-issue *and* as a "separate" hardbound monograph. (This is a format which we also call a "DocuSerial.")

"Separates" are published because specialized libraries or professionals may wish to purchase a specific thematic issue by itself in a format which can be separately cataloged and shelved, as opposed to purchasing the journal on an on-going basis. Faculty members may also more easily consider a "separate" for classroom adoption.

"Separates" are carefully classified separately with the major book jobbers so that the journal tie-in can be noted on new book order slips to avoid duplicate purchasing.

You may wish to visit Haworth's Website at . . .

http://www.HaworthPress.com

. . . to search our online catalog for complete tables of contents of these separates and related publications.

You may also call 1-800-HAWORTH (outside US/Canada: 607-722-5857), or Fax 1-800-895-0582 (outside US/Canada: 607-771-0012), or e-mail at:

getinfo@haworthpressinc.com

Trauma Practice in the Wake of September 11, 2001, edited by Steven N. Gold, PhD, and Jan Faust, PhD (Vol. 1, No. 3/4, 2002). *"Extraordinarily timely and important . . . . It is now a different world that confronts mental health professionals. This book presents both broad theoretical perspectives and the personal accounts of some who have required care and those who provide it. It begins to help us understand the changes of the post 9/11 era–how domestic terrorism has affected the national psyche as well as individuals, inflicting new wounds and awakening old hurts." (James A. Chu, MD, Director, Trauma and Dissociative Disorders Program, McLean Hospital, Belmont, Massachusetts; Editor, Journal of Trauma & Dissociation)*

Trauma Practice in the Wake of September 11, 2001

Steven N. Gold
Jan Faust
Editors

Trauma Practice in the Wake of September 11, 2001 has been co-published simultaneously as *Journal of Trauma Practice,* Volume 1, Numbers 3/4 2002.

The Haworth Maltreatment & Trauma Press
An Imprint of
The Haworth Press, Inc.
New York • London • Oxford

Published by

The Haworth Maltreatment & Trauma Press, 10 Alice Street, Binghamton, NY 13904-1580 USA

The Haworth Maltreatment & Trauma Press is an imprint of The Haworth Press, Inc., 10 Alice Street, Binghamton, NY 13904-1580 USA.

Trauma Practice in the Wake of September 11, 2001 has been co-published simultaneously as *Journal of Trauma Practice,* Volume 1, Numbers 3/4 2002.

Cover design by Lora Wiggins.

Library of Congress Cataloging-in-Publication Data

Trauma practice in the wake of September 11, 2001 / Steven N. Gold, Jan Faust, editors.
p. cm.
"Co-published simultaneously as Journal of Trauma Practice, volume 1, numbers 3/4 2002."
Includes bibliographical references and index.
ISBN 0-7890-1918-3 (alk. paper)–ISBN 0-7890-1919-1 (pbk: alk. paper)
1. Post-traumatic stress disorder 2. Stress (Psychology) 3. September 11 Terrorist Attacks, 2001–Psychological aspects 4. Traumatology 5. Terrorism. I. Gold, Steven N. II. Faust, Jan.
RC552.P67 T755 2002 2002008191
616.85′21–dc21

Indexing, Abstracting & Website/Internet Coverage

This section provides you with a list of major indexing & abstracting services. That is to say, each service began covering this periodical during the year noted in the right column. Most Websites which are listed below have indicated that they will either post, disseminate, compile, archive, cite or alert their own Website users with research-based content from this work. (This list is as current as the copyright date of this publication.)

Abstracting, Website/Indexing Coverage . . . . Year When Coverage Began

- *Cambridge Scientific Abstracts is a leading publisher of scientific information in print journals, online databases, CD-ROM and via the Internet <www.csa.com>* **2002**
- *CNPIEC Reference Guide: Chinese National Directory of Foreign Periodicals* **2001**
- *Contemporary Women's Issues* **2002**
- *Criminal Justice Abstracts* **2002**
- *Drug Policy Information Clearinghouse* **2002**
- *e-psyche, LLC <www.e-psyche.net>* **2001**
- *Family & Society Studies Worldwide <www.nisc.com>* **2001**
- *FINDEX <www.publist.com>* **2001**
- *Gay & Lesbian Abstracts provides comprehensive & in-depth coverage of the world's GLBT literature compiled by NISC & published on the Internet & CD-ROM (www.nisc.com). For more details write to: NISC, Wyman Towers, 3100 St. Paul Street, Baltimore MD 21218 USA. Phone: (+1) (410) (243-0797) FAX: (+1) (410) (243-0982). email: <sales@nisc.com>. Online: <www.nisc.com>* **2001**
- *Published International Literature on Traumatic Stress (The PILOTS Database) <www.ncptsd.org>* **2001**

(continued)

Special Bibliographic Notes related to special journal issues (separates) and indexing/abstracting:

- indexing/abstracting services in this list will also cover material in any "separate" that is co-published simultaneously with Haworth's special thematic journal issue or DocuSerial. Indexing/abstracting usually covers material at the article/chapter level.
- monographic co-editions are intended for either non-subscribers or libraries which intend to purchase a second copy for their circulating collections.
- monographic co-editions are reported to all jobbers/wholesalers/approval plans. The source journal is listed as the "series" to assist the prevention of duplicate purchasing in the same manner utilized for books-in-series.
- to facilitate user/access services all indexing/abstracting services are encouraged to utilize the co-indexing entry note indicated at the bottom of the first page of each article/chapter/contribution.
- this is intended to assist a library user of any reference tool (whether print, electronic, online, or CD-ROM) to locate the monographic version if the library has purchased this version but not a subscription to the source journal.
- individual articles/chapters in any Haworth publication are also available through the Haworth Document Delivery Service (HDDS).

To the memory of the victims of the attacks of September 11, 2001

∞ ALL HAWORTH MALTREATMENT &
TRAUMA PRESS BOOKS
AND JOURNALS ARE PRINTED
ON CERTIFIED ACID-FREE PAPER

Trauma Practice in the Wake of September 11, 2001

CONTENTS

ABOUT THE EDITORS

Steven N. Gold, PhD, earned his doctoral degree at Michigan State University in 1981, and his bachelor's degree at Washington University in St. Louis. He is Professor at Nova Southeastern University (NSU) Center for Psychological Studies, and founded and serves as Director of the Trauma Resolution and Integration Program (TRIP) at NSU's Community Mental Health Center. TRIP provides psychological services to adults experiencing difficulties related to a history of child abuse, single event trauma occurring in adulthood, or dissociative symptoms. TRIP also offers doctoral level training and conducts ongoing research on trauma-related topics. Dr. Gold's book, *Not Trauma Alone: Therapy for Child Abuse Survivors in Family and Social Context,* delineates the treatment model employed at TRIP. Dr. Gold has published and presented extensively on abuse, trauma, and dissociation. He is co-editing, along with Drs. Lenore Walker and Barbara Lucenko, a revised edition of the Handbook on Sexual Abuse of Children. He is editorial consultant and ad hoc reviewer for a number of professional journals, a Fellow of the International Society for the Study of Dissociation (ISSD), a Director on ISSD's Executive Council, and a member of the American Psychological Association, the International Society for Traumatic Stress Studies, and the National Council on Sexual Addiction and Compulsivity. He holds American Society of Clinical Hypnosis Certification in Clinical Hypnosis and is a Certified Traumatologist through Florida State University's Traumatology Institute.

Jan Faust, PhD, received her doctorate in clinical psychology from the University of Georgia after completing a Pediatric Psychology internship at University of Oklahoma Health Sciences Center. She did post-doctoral fellowship training at the Children's Hospital of Stanford University School of Medicine, after which she joined the Center for Psychological Studies faculty of Nova Southeastern University (NSU), where she is now Professor. At NSU, Dr. Faust has developed two specialty programs in the Psychology Department's Community Mental

Health Center, one of which, the Child and Adolescent Traumatic Stress Program (CATSP), is the clinical, training, and research facility serving children exposed to traumatic stressors. Dr. Faust has published scholarly work in peer-reviewed journals and book chapters in the area of child, adolescent and family psychology. Her published and presented research reflects her interest in the area of childhood stress and traumas, including interpersonal and medical traumas. Currently Dr. Faust is principal investigator on an NIMH research grant investigating the effectiveness of cognitive behavior therapy and family systems therapy for sexually abused children with PTSD. She has presented numerous papers at professional meetings such as the International Society of Traumatic Stress, the Program Evaluation and Family Violence Research International Conference, American Psychological Association, Association for the Advancement of Behavior Therapy, American Association of Marriage and Family Therapy, and American Professional Society on the Abuse of Children. In addition, she is co-editor of a book on child psychopathology and intervention to be published by Elsevier Science.

Trauma Practice in the Wake of September 11, 2001: Challenges and Opportunities

Steven N. Gold
Jan Faust

SUMMARY. The attacks of September 11th, 2001 were unprecedented in several respects. They were the first attacks on U.S. soil by a foreign power in several generations, were witnessed live on television throughout the U.S. and the world, and shattered widely held assumptions about security in the U.S. and, by implication, elsewhere. Some questions and challenges evoked by the events of September 11th of particular relevance to trauma practitioners are discussed. The contents of *Trauma Practice in the Wake of September 11, 2001*, are summarized and framed as representing a preliminary attempt to respond to some of these questions. Finally, some of the opportunities created by the September 11th attacks–increasing public awareness of trauma and its impact, fostering compassion for victims of various types of trauma, and strengthening international collaboration among traumatologists and advocates of world peace–are considered. *[Article copies available for a fee from The Haworth Document Delivery Service: 1-800-HAWORTH. E-mail address: <getinfo@haworthpressinc.com> Website: <http://www.HaworthPress.com> © 2002 by The Haworth Press, Inc. All rights reserved.]*

Steven N. Gold, PhD, and Jan Faust, PhD, are affiliated with Nova Southeastern University, Center for Psychological Studies.

[Haworth co-indexing entry note]: "Trauma Practice in the Wake of September 11, 2001: Challenges and Opportunities." Gold, Steven N., and Jan Faust. Co-published simultaneously in *Journal of Trauma Practice* (The Haworth Maltreatment & Trauma Press, an imprint of The Haworth Press, Inc.) Vol. 1, No. 3/4, 2002, pp. 1-11; and: *Trauma Practice in the Wake of September 11, 2002*. (ed: Steven N. Gold, and Jan Faust) The Haworth Maltreatment & Trauma Press, an imprint of The Haworth Press, Inc., 2001, pp. 1-11. Single or multiple copies of this article are available for a fee from The Haworth Document Delivery Service [1-800-HAWORTH, 9:00 a.m. - 5:00 p.m. (EST). E-mail address: getinfo@haworthpressinc.com].

KEYWORDS. September 11, attack, foreign power, U.S., security, trauma, practitioners, compassion, victims, collaboration, traumatologists, world peace

Several writers have suggested that a defining feature of a traumatic incident is that it is one that "shatters" an individual's basic assumptions about the nature or workings of self, others, or the world (Horowitz, 1986; Janoff-Bulman, 1992; McCann & Pearlman, 1990). For many of us, the events that occurred on the morning of September 11, 2001 were a powerful example of this characteristic of trauma. Who, upon retiring on the night of September 10, 2001, would have believed that the Pentagon, the nerve center of the armed forces of the United States, could possibly be vulnerable to direct attack? Who would have imagined it possible that the World Trade Center, the tallest structure in New York City and an impressive symbol of the financial strength of the United States, could be reduced to rubble in less than two hours time, killing thousands of people? Who would have conceived that catastrophes such as these could come to pass as the result of the coordinated simultaneous hijacking of several commercial U.S. aircraft?

In a single morning, what was previously unfathomable to many people became a reality. Events such as these would have assailed the sense of safety of people anywhere they might have occurred. They were, however, probably even more shocking to the people of the United States than they would have been to the citizens of most other countries because they were so inconceivable. The last direct attack on U.S. soil, Pearl Harbor, took place two to three generations ago, far from the continental U.S. Before that, it had been well over a century since a foreign power had attacked U.S. soil. Consequently, it has long been part of the national consciousness that war and attacks from abroad occur in other countries, but not in the U.S. On September 11th, 2001, this assumption was instantaneously and thoroughly obliterated.

These events were also unprecedented in that they were witnessed "live" on television by millions from where they were actually occurring. This raises the question of whether the DSM-IV (American Psychiatric Association, 1994) criterion A for diagnosing Posttraumatic Stress Disorder (PTSD)–witnessing death–applies here. Can viewing the sudden catastrophic murder of thousands of innocent civilians in real time on television engender posttraumatic symptoms or even diagnosable PTSD?

In the days following September 11th, as the lines of communication between New York City and the rest of the country gradually were re-established, anecdotal reports revealed that many New Yorkers had no idea how powerfully the attacks had impacted the rest of the country. The situation was viewed by many New Yorkers as being analogous to the 1997 bombing of the U.S. federal building in Oklahoma City in that they were seen primarily as constituting a local catastrophe. Many in New York City did not appreciate the degree to which the entire country had been affected. It was a surprise to many New Yorkers, for example, to discover that in the days following September 11th regular television programming across the country was abandoned in favor of around the clock coverage of the attacks and their aftermath.

In parallel fashion, in the weeks and months following September 11th, it has become progressively clear that the shock of the events of that day was not confined to those in the United States. It was apparently not only U.S. citizens who had presumed that the U.S. was invulnerable to the types of attacks that occurred on September 11th. Many people around the world appear to have shared this assumption. As a result, they not only felt tremendous concern and sympathy for those directly affected in the U.S., but found their beliefs about their own level of safety and security intensely shaken. If the U.S. could be assaulted in this fashion, they seemed to conclude, then any country was subject to being similarly assaulted.

THE CHALLENGES

As many have already noted, the events of September 11th ushered in a new era. The attacks on the Pentagon and the World Trade Center, and the subsequent threat of acts of biological, chemical, and nuclear warfare, immediately and drastically created a shift in perspective among people around the globe. The constantly looming specter of sudden, large-scale terrorist assaults arouses the potential for a type of trauma that is relatively new and about which, therefore, little is known. Traumatologists were just beginning to refine their understanding of how to effectively respond to disasters such as those that occurred at

Columbine High School and in Oklahoma City. Suddenly, we are now confronted with the potential for a different type of catastrophic situation that is vastly greater in both scope and duration.

Despite the extensive empirical and clinical literature on trauma that has accumulated in the past quarter century, it is evident that our existing knowledge base on trauma will need to be expanded in order to adequately address the challenges unique to the ongoing threat of wide spread terrorist attacks. There is still considerable controversy about how, when, or to some degree even whether it is productive to proactively provide services aimed at the prevention of posttraumatic stress disorder such as Critical Incident Stress Debriefing (CISD). Events such as the attacks on the World Trade Center and Pentagon, and the subsequent anthrax scare, confront us with a situation that raises even more ambiguous issues. It is widely accepted by the general public, and validated by government officials and the news media, that these incidents signal the existence of a very real threat of future attacks that could occur just about any place in the United States or abroad at any time.

In the face of this unprecedented set of circumstances, an entirely new and pressing series of questions has suddenly emerged. Many of these issues are so novel that they are just beginning to be articulated. Some of the more salient questions raised by the September 11th attacks are:

> How can we best help those most directly affected by terrorist attacks, such as the immediate family of those killed and injured, and emergency service workers who respond at the scene of the attack, to cope with and recover from the effects of this form of trauma?

> How do the forms of assistance required immediately following incidents of this type differ from those needed months and years later?

> To what extent, if at all, does living with the continuous threat of terrorist attacks carry the potential to adversely affect psychological adjustment?

Are there preventative measures or coping strategies that can lessen or eliminate the potentially psychologically debilitating impact of living under the ongoing threat of terrorism?

What particular risks do these circumstances pose for the psychological well being of children, and how can their potential adverse impact be attenuated?

Can repeated exposure to depictions of terrorist threats and attacks in the news media increase the incidence of PTSD and other trauma-related disorders in the general population or in particular at-risk sub-groups?

Can the way in which security measures against terrorist threats are implemented affect whether the prevalence and intensity of traumatic stress are exacerbated or ameliorated?

What are the psychological costs of issuing non-specific announcements that a terrorist attack might be immanent, and are they outweighed by the practical benefits of alerting the public to be more vigilant for signs of potential danger than usual?

IN THIS COLLECTION: BEGINNING TO MEET THE CHALLENGE

The lead sentence of the abstract of our editorial in the first issue of the *Journal of Trauma Practice* (*JTP*) read, "In the new and evolving field of traumatology, the need to keep practitioners apprised of emerging developments is acute" (Gold & Faust, 2002, p. 1). Chillingly, these words are even truer now than they were when they were written. In light of *JTP*'s mission, the timely dissemination of knowledge to trauma practitioners, it seems particularly appropriate that the Journal address the issues raised by the events of September 11th.

Figuring out how to find reliable sources for this type of information, however, was neither a simple nor an obvious task. On one hand, the existing knowledge base to answer questions such as those listed above is extremely spotty at best. On the other hand, there is a real and pressing need to begin the process of gathering the provisional information that is available to help address these issues and making it readily accessible to trauma practitioners.

The current volume, therefore, must undeniably be considered merely an initial attempt to address some of the questions listed above. We urge the reader to keep in mind that the information provided here is provisional. Much of what is presented here represents the earliest stages of investigation into questions such as those posed above. The field of traumatology has been criticized in the past for adhering to information and methods that were not adequately empirically validated. It is essential to remember that the initial phases of study by necessity precede empirical validation, and that in the interim the practical needs of afflicted individuals cannot be ignored until our initial observations are subjected to full empirical testing. However, it is equally vital that our preliminary understanding about new areas of study be recognized as such, so that it does not prematurely calcify into rigidly adhered-to dogma. It is in this spirit that we caution our readers to be cognizant that much of the material that appears in this volume is likely in time to be significantly revised or refuted as it is subjected to empirical scrutiny. Nonetheless, we believe the content of this volume constitutes a promising beginning to addressing the psychological needs of the new era initiated by the September 11th attacks.

Charles R. Figley and his colleagues, Kathleen Regan Figley and James Norman, share their experiences providing mental health services to the emergency service workers who responded to the destruction of the World Trade Center (WTC). As administrators of Green Cross Projects (GCP), probably the foremost organization designed to provide psychological services at the sites of catastrophic events, they are exceptionally well-equipped to speak to the issue of how to effectively respond in such circumstances. They describe how GCP mobilized and responded to the WTC disaster, review the outcomes of GCP's services there, and discuss their initial conclusions about how to best deliver mental health relief services in response to this type of attack.

J. Eric Gentry, a former doctoral student of Charles Figley who now is co-director of the International Traumatology Institute at the University of South Florida, also participated in the relief efforts at the WTC. He has worked extensively in the area of compassion fatigue, the adverse impact on practitioners of engaging in trauma work. He writes here about compassion fatigue and its impact on professionals who work with traumatized individuals and groups, and offers recommendations on how to prevent it, attenuate its effects, and recover from it. Included are his description of how his experiences responding to the WTC disaster have broadened his own subjective understanding of compassion fatigue and of how to effectively cope with and overcome it.

We initially contacted Lenore Meldrum, a traumatologist from Australia, to conduct an interview for this volume. Although she agreed to take on this task, she proposed and volunteered to carry out another project as well. She felt it was crucial that this collection include explicit recognition that although the events of September 11th occurred in the U.S., they have made a profound impression throughout the international community. Consequently, Ms. Meldrum took it upon herself to invite traumatologists from around the world to comment on the effects the attacks have had in their own countries. Their responses comprise the final piece in this section.

The newness of the phenomenon of ongoing terrorist threat made it particularly challenging to promptly obtain reliable information for this issue on terrorism and it impact. Our solution to this dilemma was to identify experts on terrorism and arrange interviews with them. We have been able to enlist the participation of three individuals uniquely qualified to knowledgably address the topic of terrorism: Jerrold M. Post, Eyad El-Sarraj and Ofra Ayalon.

Too often professionals in trauma practitioners are extremely familiar with the impact of interpersonal violence on victims, but have only cursory awareness of the literature on perpetrators of violence. We are better equipped to help the victims of acts of terrorism when we have some understanding of the mentality and motivations of those who carry out these attacks. Jerrold M. Post, who is unquestionably in the forefront of those scholar-practitioners examining the psychology of terrorism, is interviewed on that topic by *JTP* Co-Editor Steven N. Gold.

Frequent news reports of terrorist attacks in Israel made that country an obvious place to focus our search for expertise on the psychological consequences of living with the ongoing threat of terrorism. When Eyad El-Sarraj, a Palestinian psychiatrist, first arrived in Gaza, he was the only psychiatrist in that region of Israel. For over ten years now has been providing mental health services there. He is interviewed by Australian traumatologist Lenore Meldrum about the effects that the constant threat of terrorism has had on the Palestinian people of Israel.

Frances S. Waters is a social worker who on several occasions has been sent abroad by the U.S. Government to consult on the effects of trauma, particularly on children, adolescents, and families. Although she is from the U.S., her ancestry is Lebanese. She interviewed Ofra Ayalon, an Israeli psychologist whose work has also focused on the sequelae of trauma in children, adolescents, and families. Their discussion centers on the impact that terrorism has had on Jews in Israel.

Although relatively little research exists regarding the impact of terrorism on children, even less is available which examines the psychological aftermath of terrorism on children residing in the United States. What we do know about children's responses to acts of terrorism is that they differ from those of adults, and developmental status and changes can influence children's trauma responses to a great degree. Robin H. Gurwitch, and Betty Pfefferbaum, both of the University of Oklahoma Health Sciences Center, in collaboration with Michael J. T. Leftwich of Emporia State University, report on these developmental differences, based on data from the bombing of the Murrah federal building in Oklahoma City, in their paper "The Impact of Terrorism on Children: Considerations for a New Era." A key example of the differences between adult and childhood trauma reactions is that children tend to express their trauma responses through the exhibition of salient regressive behaviors and engagement in play with trauma themes. In fact, not only do children experience trauma symptoms that differ in quality from their adult counterparts, but there appear to be some age differences in trauma reactions within the child survivor domain as well. Gurwitch and her colleagues found that sleep disturbances and self-regulation issues were more problematic in infants than in other age groups of children. The elucidation of developmental differences in children's reactions to terrorist attacks is key in planning for appropriate intervention and treatment. The enormity of the September 11th bombing of the WTC has obscured in the minds of many that this was not the first WTC terrorist attack.

JoAnn Difede and David Eskra, two psychologists affiliated with New York Presbyterian Hospital, present a case study of the treatment of a survivor of the 1993 WTC bombing. Their outcome assessments at admission, periodically during treatment, at termination, and at follow-up, support the efficacy of Cognitive Processing therapy for survivors of terrorist assaults with posttraumatic stress disorder.

OPPORTUNITIES

The September 11th attacks differ in some substantial ways from an organized effort by a large foreign military. Given the fact that only a couple dozen of people carried out such massive destruction in the terrorist attacks, personal safety and security seem even more precarious than in international war. It will be interesting to see if healing and the resolution of trauma symptoms is enhanced by the national unification of people across the U.S. Do the huge number of cars bearing flags, people wearing ribbons, and increased social cohesion on a national scale bolster recovery? The level and pervasiveness of unification that have arisen in response to the events of September 11th have not been seen in other disasters. Although media coverage has been observed to promote trauma reactions through vicarious retraumatization (Gurwitch et al., 1999), it also may have some beneficial effects in the healing process; shared experiences and the common resolve to stand together in the face of adversity can enhance locus of control.

Many trauma practitioners, especially those in the mental health professions, have had extensive experience with forms of trauma that most commonly occur within the confines of domestic settings–childhood sexual and physical abuse, partner battering, elder abuse. It is disheartening to many of us that the larger society is slow to recognize the reality of, prevalence of, and toll taken by these forms of interpersonal violence. At times it has seemed as if the popular media have been more receptive to claims that allegations of the perpetration of violence are false and to accusations that victims of maltreatment exaggerate the ill effects they have suffered than to recognizing the very real damage done by interpersonal violence. Repeatedly we encounter evidence supporting the frequently quoted observation of psychiatrist Judith Herman (1992) that

> It is very tempting to take the side of the perpetrator. All the perpetrator asks is that the bystander do nothing. He appeals to the universal desire to see, hear, and speak no evil. The victim, on the contrary, asks the bystander to share the burden of pain. The victim demands action, engagement, and remembering. (p. 7).

In stark contrast to the fate of many survivors of domestic violence and abuse, who have been abandoned and even denigrated by the larger society, the victims of the terrorist attacks of September 11th have enjoyed the heartfelt support of their families, their communities, the country as a whole, and, indeed the world. Undoubtedly they have benefited from the social support that empirical research has repeatedly demonstrated mitigates the adverse effects of traumatic events. No one dared to suggest, or even to consider, that the pain of the victims of the

September 11th attacks was imagined or exaggerated. We all felt vulnerable, and we therefore all experienced some of the horror and dread aroused by the threat of terrorism.

One of the opportunities presented by the horrific events of September 11th is the possibility that it may help to raise public consciousness about the reality of and psychological cost extracted by traumatic events. We can only hope that this depth and breadth of this experience throughout our society will foster greater sensitivity for the plight of those subjected to trauma in more private, less visible circumstances. In order to fully discharge our responsibility to the survivors we serve, trauma practitioners carry the obligation to do what we can to make this possibility an actuality.

In addition, this event may serve to increase our nation's sense of compassion for other nations that have not previously been as fortunate to escape terrorism on homeland soil as has the United States. The notion that one of the world's leading powers is not invulnerable only further heightens fear of susceptibility to terrorist attacks, regardless from which country one hails. This together with Americans' increased empathy for those from other countries exposed to terrorism can serve to foster unity across nations, ideally promulgating the concept of world peace.

Another prospect created by the terrorist attacks of September 11th is to create stronger ties among traumatologists from different cultures, with divergent political affiliations, and from diverse regions of the world. In compiling this volume we have been privileged to witness what we hope comprise the beginnings of an ongoing process toward that end. One of the more salient examples of this trend are the statements from traumatologists from various countries about the impact of the September 11th attacks in their own lands.

Another is the empathic bond formed between Frances Waters and Ofra Ayalon during their interview on the impact of terrorism on children, adults, and families. Although they had never met before, during their interview, conducted via an intercontinental long distance telephone call, they rapidly developed a sense of solidarity in their shared concern for the welfare of traumatized children and their families. We fervently hope that the events of September 11th will promote the formation of connections such as these among the international community of traumatologists. Setting an example for this type of communication and collaboration may ultimately be one of the most powerful steps we can take toward ending the cycle of violence, whether on an international scale, or within the intimate circle of the family.

REFERENCES

American Psychiatric Association. (1994). *Diagnostic and statistical manual of mental disorders* (4th ed.). Washington, DC: American Psychiatric Association.

Gurwitch, R.H., Leftwich, M.J.T., Cote, M., Messenbaugh, A., & Pfefferbaum, B. (1999, November). *Media impact on PTSD symptoms in young children following disasters*. J. Faust (Chair). Symposium on Models for Understanding Children's Reaction and Recovery to Diverse Traumas. Presented at the Meeting of International Society of Trauma Stress Studies, Miami, FL.

Herman, J.L. (1992). *Trauma and recovery: The aftermath of violence–From domestic abuse to political terror*. New York: Basic Books.

Horowitz, M.J. (1986). *Stress response syndromes* (2nd ed.) Northvale, NJ: Jason Aronson.

Janoff-Bulman, R. (1992). *Shattered assumptions: Towards a new psychology of trauma*. New York: Free Press.

McCann, L., & Pearlman, L.A. (1990). *Psychological trauma and the adult survivor: Theory, treatment, and transformation*. Philadelphia: Brunner/Mazel.

Tuesday Morning September 11, 2001: The Green Cross Projects' Role as a Case Study in Community-Based Traumatology Services

Charles R. Figley
Kathleen Regan Figley
James Norman

SUMMARY. This article sites several post-attack, national surveys indicating negative mental health consequences as a context for considering the recent mobilization of the Green Cross Projects (GCP) in New York's lower Manhattan area. The GCP is a humanitarian, disaster mental health organization that provides crisis intervention to organizations

---

Charles R. Figley, PhD, is Professor and Director, Florida State University Traumatology Institute and Founder of the Green Cross Projects, 2407 C University Center, Tallahassee, FL 32306-2570.

Kathleen Regan Figley, MS, is Executive Vice President, Green Cross Foundation, Immediate Past-President of the Green Cross Projects (2000-2001), and Incident Commander of the New York Green Cross Project (2001), 4244 West Tennessee Street, #386, Tallahassee, FL 32304 (E-mail: cfigley@mailer.fsu.edu).

James Norman, MEd, is Former Director of Operation Heartland, President of the Green Cross Projects (2001-2002) and Incident Commander of the New York Green Cross Project (2001).

Address correspondence to: Charles R. Figley, PhD, Professor and Director, Florida State University Traumatology Institute, Founder, Green Cross Projects, 2407 C University Center, Tallahassee, FL 32306-2570 (E-mail: Cfigley@garnet.acns.fsu.edu).

[Haworth co-indexing entry note]: "Tuesday Morning September 11, 2001: The Green Cross Projects' Role as a Case Study in Community-Based Traumatology Services." Figley, Charles R., Kathleen Regan Figley, and James Norman. Co-published simultaneously in *Journal of Trauma Practice*. (The Haworth Maltreatment & Trauma Press, an imprint of The Haworth Press, Inc.) Vol. 1, No. 3/4, 2002, pp. 13-36; and: *Trauma Practice in the Wake of September 11, 2001* (ed: Steven Gold, and Jan Faust) The Haworth Maltreatment & Trauma Press, an imprint of The Haworth Press, Inc., 2001, pp. 13-36. Single or multiple copies of this article are available for a fee from The Haworth Document Delivery Service [1-800-HAWORTH, 9:00 a.m. - 5:00 p.m. (EST). E-mail address: getinfo@haworthpressinc.com].

(public and private) affected by traumatic events. After noting the history, purpose, and structure of the GCP, the article describes its recently completed mobilization beginning with the invitation by a large, local service employee union. Based on the invitation an agreed upon mission was established with six measurable objectives. This is followed by a description of what happened, who and how many were served and trained. The final section of the paper discusses the lessons applied from traumatology and the lessons learned that should be applied to future community-based, organizational assistance following a major disaster.

KEYWORDS. Attack, national surveys, mental health, Green Cross Projects, GCP, New York, Manhattan, humanitarian, disaster, crisis interventions, traumatic events, traumatology, community, assistance

At 8:45AM on September 11th in the first year of the millennia America's sense of security was changed forever. American Airlines Flight 11, a Boeing 767 carrying 92 people, crashed into the World Trade Center's North Tower. Eighteen minutes later United Airlines Flight 175, also a Boeing 767, with 65 people aboard also crashed into the World Trade Center at the South Tower. Two other tragedies were about to happen involving two other locations and two other planes. Everyone in lower Manhattan was focused on the horror of the Trade Center towers.

Fifteen blocks away at the Service Employee International Union Local 32B-J building on Avenue of the Americas at Grand Street, over 800 union *staff* (those who administer programs for the union members) watched in horror. Most witnessed dozens of people jump from the Towers to their death, the stream of rescue workers responding to the disaster, the stream of people running from the towers, and then the collapse of the Towers onto these brave responders and so many others. Local 32BJ union *members* are building service workers, i.e., janitors, window cleaners, elevator operators, and security guards. More than 1500 members of 32B-J worked in the World Trade Towers. Another 7500 members were working in Manhattan below 14th Street, blocks from Ground Zero. Not only was 32B-J suffering its worst single day of loss of life, its union members, professional staff, managers, and general staff were in emotional shock. They required a massive assistance effort. Through professional connections they learned of the Green Cross Projects and requested immediate assistance.

In a September 14th letter to the Green Cross Founder (first author) and current President (second author) requesting assistance, Mary Ellen Boyd, the Chief Executive Officer of the Union's Health Fund, explained the situation described above, and noted that

> We have a small Employee Assistance staff and a group of volunteer therapists to help us deal with the situation but we are totally without expertise.

Her letter went on to say:

> Your assistance would be invaluable. Our employees and members are suffering with many different symptoms and their families are reporting difficulties as well. To add to our complications, will be the economic realities our members will be facing.

Ms. Boyd herself would be forced out of her residence because it was in the blast area near the World Trade Center.

PROXIMAL VERSUS DISTAL IMPACT

Most people recall easily where they were and what they were doing when they learned of the September 11th terrorist attack. It is one of the darkest days in the history of humankind and certainly the United States. To purposefully kill so many innocent people in such a dramatic way changes the formula for how Americans calculate a sense of safety, security, and freedom. The subsequent threats of bioterrorism and the emerging troop deployments and military actions against the Taliban in Afghanistan make it all the more obvious that we are now in a new era.

What are the varying degrees of impact of this terrorist event, depending upon where one lives? Figley (2002) has noted how the Perpetrator-Innocence-Connectedness (PIC) score can be applied to answering the question. Developed as a shorthand way of estimating the degree of distress that groups may experience from a specific traumatic event (Figley, 1985), the score is only a rough measure and does not take into account the cumulative effects of traumatic events. As illustrated in Table 1, the PIC score is an estimate of the magnitude of challenges in coping with a

TABLE 1. The Perpetrator-Innocence-Connectedness (PIC) Score

		Degree of Innonence of Victims		
		Low (job-related) (1-5)	Medium (civilians) (6-10)	High (Children) (11-15)
Degree of Perpetration as Perceived by the Victimized	HIGH (5) (Terrorism)			
	MEDIUM HIGH (4) (Violent Crime)			
	MEDIUM (3) (Malfeasant Accidents)			
	MEDIUM LOW (2) (accidents)			
	LOW (1) (Natural Disasters)			

Connectedness: 5 = No connectedness, 4 = Very vague, 3 = Moderate, 2 = High, 1 = Very High

particular traumatic event and is determined by simply multiplying the innocence factor (1-15) by the perpetrator factor (1-5) and dividing by the connectedness factor (1-5).

In contrast to a natural disaster, which is random and unpreventable (Doherty, 1999), terrorist acts are purposeful and can be directed at everyone present, including innocent children. In contrast to a natural disaster in which few, if any, died, the terrorist acts on September 11 may have killed as many as 6,000, including children and other innocent people. However, one of the most important differences between a natural disaster and a terrorist act is the connectedness factor. The connectedness factor, which is determined by estimating how much the respondent identifies with the helpless and victimized, can greatly affect the degree to which one feels traumatized. High identification, including those with relatives and friends who died, would be the most difficult to overcome.

In general, human-caused trauma engenders more psychological harm than natural disasters and accidents (Figley, in press). Those affected realize that their traumatization experiences could have been prevented, and that is what makes the event and its impact harder to accept. When victims are specifically targeted, it makes it difficult to come to terms with the traumatic event. The most difficult trauma to overcome, however, is being "caught in the crossfire," because the situation could have been prevented and because the intended target was someone else. This is the case in the instances of terrorism.

The new period initialed by the attacks of September 11th is marked by the experience of heightened levels of fear, uncertainty, and insecurity by a large number of Americans (Institute for Social Research, 2001). In a recent survey of American consumers the University of Michigan Social Research Institute found that although more than half reported that the terrorist attacks had no effect on them, a larger than expected number said otherwise. About 20 percent of all consumers surveyed between Sept. 15 and Oct. 7 reported that their sense of personal safety was shaken a "great deal" by the attacks, and 29 percent reported that it was shaken "a good amount." As we would expect given the location of the attacks, the eastern US was more affected: 24 percent of the residents of the Northeast and Southern regions reported that their sense of personal safety was shaken a great deal, compared to 14 percent of residents of the West and North Central regions.

A series of nationwide telephone surveys, conducted by the Princeton Survey Research Associates (2001) for the Pew Research Center (*http://www.people-press.org/midoct01que.htm*), found that although depression, sleeplessness, and fear were high immediately following the September 11th attack, the majority of Americans have recovered. In mid-September, 71% of those polled agreed with the statement that "In the past few days, have you yourself felt depressed because of your concerns about terrorist attacks or the war against terrorism?" By early October the number who said "yes" dropped to 42%. A month later only 31% answered replied affirmatively to this question.

Similarly, in Mid-September 33% answered, "yes" to the question. "In the past few days, have you had any trouble sleeping because of your concerns about terrorist attacks or the war against terrorism?" The percentage dropped to 18% in early October , and in the latest surveys conducted in mid-October, the percentage is only 13%. Yet the percentage of those who are "very worried" that "there will soon be another terrorist attack in the US" appears relatively unchanged since the question was first posed in early October. At that time 28% were "very worried" and 45% reported they were "somewhat worried." In mid-October 27% responded as "very worried" and 40% "somewhat worried."[1] Another survey found similar patterns of response (PSRA, 2001).

It was within this cultural context that the Green Cross Projects was contacted to help out in New York City. The purpose of this article is to describe how one group of trauma practitioners responded to requests for assistance from New York immediately following the attack. The way in which this response was informed by the existing knowledge base in traumatology, and what we can learn from it that can be applied to future catastrophic incidents, are highlighted.

GREEN CROSS PROJECTS' RESPONSE

The Green Cross Projects is a membership-based, humanitarian assistance program providing traumatology services to individuals, groups, and communities recovering from disasters and other traumatic events. The Green Cross Projects (GCP), was established in response to another terrorist attack in the US, the Oklahoma City bombing of 1995 (Figley, 1995). Since that time GCP has responded to events that have included a website for the war in Bosnia (1996), the responders to the Port Arthur shootings in Tasmania (1996), South Africa's Truth and Reconciliation Commission (1996), services and consultation for the State of Florida (Tropical Storm Josephine, 1996-1997), consultation on the Arkadelphia Arkansas tornado (1997), consultation on Northern Ireland (1999 and 2001), consultation on the Littleton, Colorado (Columbine) Shooting (1999), consultation on the war in Kosovo (2000), consultation and full mobilization in response to the terrorist attacks on New York City (2001).

The President of the GCP is responsible for recognizing that disaster of sufficient magnitude may require the services of the GCP and places the organization on standby status. As a result a cascade of actions are set in motion to alert the GCP membership of the event, inquire about membership availability to serve, and alert potential hosts in the affected area of the GCP services available.

Mobilization is also declared by the President of the GCP based on (a) a specific invitation from a host organization, (b) a specific and attainable Project Mission is identified through interaction with the host, (c) availability of sufficient resources and members, and (d) identification of key individuals to serve in the key disaster services roles.

Consistent with disaster management protocol, there was an Incident Commander (initially the second author and later the third author), Operations Manager (the second author), public relations specialist (the first author), team leaders with five service providers for each team.

The Incident Commander (IC) is in charge of the Green Cross Project deployment cadre and is the supervisor for the Operations Manager, the Public Relations Specialist, and the team leaders. The IC follows a standard protocol for the operation, maintains a daily log, and is the point of contact (systems interface) with the host organization (sponsor).

The Operations Manager (OM) is responsible for the day-to-day service provision during the mobilization. This includes but is not limited to insuring that all service-related paper work is completed, all logistics and planning is complete, and all transportation needs are coordinated. The OM serves as the assistant to the IC and represents the IC and performs all other duties specified by the IC.

The Public Relations Specialist is responsible for representing the Green Cross Project (mobilization) to all entities outside the operation. This includes the news media, other organizations involved in the operation, and the general public.

These roles are consistent with the incident command structure utilized by most disaster-oriented organizations. Unlike other organizations, however, the GCP operations manual requires that all teams also included a compassion fatigue specialist (see Gentry, this volume) responsible for debriefing, defusing and the general morale of the team.

In anticipation of the request for services, the second author placed the GCP on standby and identified two teams of 6 members who were prepared to go immediately to New York. Two compassion fatigue specialists were among the team members. After the September 14th letter was received by the GCP, the second author declared the mobilization, established the New York Green Cross Project, dispatched the advanced party of GCP workers to arrive September 16th and begin providing services the next day following an orientation by the Incident Commander. The Incident Commander had met with the Host (32B-J) the previous evening and together they established the full mission of the mobilization for the NYGCP.

It is vital that the GCP or any organization providing assistance be very clear about what the affected community needs and wants. Immediately following the Oklahoma City bombing in 1995, for example, the first author met with public and private officials to determine what would be most needed by those responsible for helping the bombing victims, their families, the rescue workers, and other affected. It was determined that training was the most acute need.

Within a few months, more than 1,000 professionals received at least one workshop of training and fifty-eight completed the entire five-course program of training and received a certificate as a Registered Traumatologist (Figley, 1998).

Those Registered Traumatologists became the founding members of the Green Cross Projects (GCP) and were ready to apply the lessons they had learned both in the classroom and in their own State in helping people recover from terrorist attacks. As it turned out, Oklahoma sent one of the largest contingents of traumatologists to New York, second only to Florida.

The program of training they completed was adopted by the Florida State University's Traumatology Institute as the Certified Traumatologist certificate program (Figley, 1998). Over the years the Institute established three other certifications: Master Traumatologist, Field Traumatologist, and Compassion Fatigue Specialist. With certification comes automatic membership in GCP.

Members practice traumatology guided by the Academy of Traumatology standards of practice and ethical guidelines (Academy of Traumatology, 1999). The Standards are located at the Green Cross Foundation's web site at (*http://www.greencross.org*). Since June of 1998 a Board of Directors has governed the GCP. In addition to an annual meeting, a web site (*http://www.fsu.edu/~gcp/*) informs members throughout the world. During the New York City mobilization, for example, there were updates on what was happening, copies of various messages to members, press releases, news accounts, and other helpful information for those who were activated as well as others who were interested. Also, members receive the international journal *Traumatology* in both written and virtual form at (*http:// www.fsu.edu/~trauma/*).

The Mission of the GCP is to provide immediate trauma intervention to all areas of the world when a crisis occurs either through its members individually or through mobilization (World Health Organization, 1997). Most often GCP members provide humanitarian service in their local communities. However, GCP is unique in its ability to activate large numbers of members to respond to major disasters, such as the one that affected the island of Manhattan, New York City on 11 September.

Deployment Mission

The Mission of any GCP deployment is to transform Victims into Survivors. Victims may have a sense of helplessness that limits their ability to cope with future events, traumatic or otherwise. Survivors, on the other hand, use lessons learned from the traumatic event to heal and become stronger as a result. Immediately following a traumatic event victims struggle to address five fundamental questions (Figley, 1985):

1. What happened to me (us)? This question can be applied to oneself, one's family, company, neighborhood, city, or country. This question is the most fundamental one in the processing of trauma mem-

ories and is associated with the experience of shock, disbelief, disorientation, and confusion. GCP service providers help clients to recognize what *has* happened to them. Most often this is achieved by encouraging them to talk about their experiences or to depict them in some other way such as through the modalities used in expressive therapies (e.g., poetry, drawings).

2. Why did it happen to me (us)? This question is at the heart of one's sense of responsibility for either the cause or consequences of the event, or both. Survivors often associate their actions preceding the traumatic event with feelings of guilt. This was certainly the case with those who had worked in or near Ground Zero. GCP service providers create an opportunity for the traumatized to re-evaluate their actions,
3. Why did I (we) do what I (we) did during and right after this disaster? This second-guessing and self-analysis is central to acquiring some degree of mastery over the memories and events that were or still are traumatic. GCP service providers gently encourage survivors to address such difficult and often troubling thoughts associated with self-evaluation. Often hearing other survivors talk about their misgivings enable them to reassure the others while, at the same time, reassuring themselves.
4. Why have I (we) acted as I (we) have since the disaster? This question represents an effort to self-assess to determine if what is being experienced is cause for alarm and requires the help of others. It also suggests that the need for mastery of what may be described as being obsessed with the traumatic event. GCP service providers conduct a wide variety and large number of public education sessions that discuss the immediate and long-term psychosocial consequences and opportunities following dangerous and horrifying events. These sessions not only address how to handle these responses as a survivor, but also how to help friends and family to differentiate what are normal reactions and coping from effects that require more attention and perhaps professional assistance.
5. Will I (we) be able to cope if this disaster happens again? The response to this fundamental question is an indication of if and how much the survivor has learned from the trauma and its wake. The answer to this and the other questions discussed above forms the survivor's "healing theory" (Figley, 1985; 1989) and enables him or her to move on with life and let go of the emotional reactions as-

sociated with the memories. This last question is the most challenging for GCP service providers because only time and extensive discussion and processing enable survivors to develop their own healing theory.

Standard Mobilization Procedures

The GCP works with the host or client to clarify the mission of the deployment and specify measurable and attainable goals. Typically the services provided are provided in waves:

Wave I (Days 1-10 following the disaster): Crisis stabilization, contacting local GCP members to establish a chapter for continuity of care.

Wave II (Days 5-15): Stress management, social support, and orientation of Management.

Wave III (Days 10-20): All the above plus training, assessment and referral, and family resource development.

Wave IV (Days 15-40): All the above services plus grief and loss consultation and counseling.

Specific Services Provided

The GCP responds to requests from individuals, organizations, and other entities following a traumatic event. The requests can include any or all of the following:

1. Crisis assistance and counseling: helping those in shock get back on their feet and access their natural coping methods and resources.
2. Assessment and referral services: identifying who is recovering properly from the traumatic event, who is not, why they are not recovering and what additional or other services are needed when and by whom.
3. Orientation and consultation to management: educating management about the immediate, week-to-week, and long term consequences of traumatic events for individuals, work groups, families, and larger systems.

4. Training, education, and certification: preparing management, human resources, employee assistance professionals, and service providers with sufficient guidance and competence to first do no harm to the traumatized and help them recover.
5. Family resource management designing and implementing programs for strengthening and promoting family wellness in the wake of traumatic events, with special attention to young children.
6. Long-term trauma counseling: helping those unable to recover quickly from the trauma by providing individual and group trauma and grief counseling.

These services are provided over varying periods of time and performed initially by members of a deployment team. TGCP service providers are transported into the impacted area within hours after the request is made. They stay from between 3 to 6 weeks or until local GCP members can relieve them.

THE TERRORIST ATTACK AND THE NEW YORK CITY GCP MOBILIZATION

Initial Mission, Objectives and Outcome

Prior to the initiation of services for the Host (i.e., Local 32 B-J) it was agreed that the Mission of the Green Cross New York Project at 32B-J is to help the management, staff, employees, and membership mitigate the impact of traumatic response induced by the September 11, 2001 attack on the World Trade Center. To accomplish this mission, Green Cross New York Project developed the objectives outlined below. While the Host has and will benefit from all the objectives, the first three are most relevant to their immediate needs.

Objective #1: Provide immediate critical incident stress management and crisis-oriented services utilizing: scheduled group defusing/educational sessions with fund and union staff; scheduled individual defusing/educational sessions with fund, union staff and members; unscheduled individual and/or group sessions with fund, union staff and members, and crisis interventions as needed.

Outcome: Green Cross Traumatologist volunteers facilitated 76 group defusing/educational sessions from September 17 through October 14, 2001 with the fund and union staff. The length of group sessions ranged from one to one and a half hours with 2 sessions going for 4 hours. Total attendance for group sessions was 635.

Green Cross Traumatologist volunteers facilitated individual defusing/crisis interventions from September 17 through October 14, 2001 with fund, union staff, and members. The length of individual sessions usually ranged from 20 minutes to 1 hour but on occasion ran longer. There were 2,159 individual defusing/crisis interventions. Individuals with more than critical needs were referred to their Employee Assistance Program so those needs could be met. There were approximately 30 referrals to EAP by GCP personnel. The 32B-J EAP employees were a tremendous help to our GCP volunteers. The total number of GCP contacts with 32B-J staff and members was 2,794.

Green Cross Project trauma specialists' primary function on a deployment is to assess, stabilize, and refer as needed. During the assessment and stabilization process at 32B-J, more specific needs were discovered. The family members that had lost loved ones in the attack on the World Trade Center Towers faced a very difficult situation. Most of them will not have the body of their loved one for formal final services. This usually results in an ambiguous loss process. Dr. Pauline Boss from the University of Minnesota is an expert in helping family members process through ambiguous loss. Dr. Boss brought two teams of ambiguous loss experts from her program to New York City to work with affected 32B-J families.

The first team of four ambiguous loss specialists and Dr. Boss were on site from September 26 through 29, 2001. While on site, the team was able to identify family members that had lost loved ones and helped them begin processing through their ambiguous grief. The University of Minnesota team was able to contact and assist four family members during their first deployment.

During the University of Minnesota's second deployment, from October 10 through 14, 2001, Dr. Boss and a team of four held a training program on ambiguous loss. Twenty-three local mental health professionals attended the training. This training was put to use on Saturday October 14, 2001, when eight families were brought together at 32B-J to begin developing their support system. Approximately 25 adults and 10 children attended this session. Feedback from the family members in attendance was positive indicating that this session was much needed and they would like to have more in the future.

Objective #2: Provide a five-hour course in basic care for the traumatized to 100 licensed mental health providers who will form the basis for a referral networking system working with the Employee Assistance Program at 32B-J. Provide additional courses on traumatology as needed and requested.

Outcome: Green Cross Project trainers provided four sixteen-hour trainings for certification as Registered Traumatologist to 69 mental health professionals. The professionals trained were identified by the Host (Local 32 B-J) through their EAP provider network. Although GCP had set a goal of 100 trained traumatologists, the Host was satisfied that the number of providers trained (69) would be able to sufficiently manage union staff and members' needs in the short term. GCP offered to provide additional training sessions if so identified by the Host. Training included basic care for the traumatized, as well as self-care for the mental health professionals while working with the traumatized. Of those mental health professionals, 45 are part of 32B-J's Employee Assistance Program. The other 24 have indicated that they will volunteer their services to 32B-J as needed.

The first training was held at 32B-J during the week of September 23rd through 29th, with 6 trainees, 4 from 32B-J EAP and 2 volunteers. The second training, also at 32B-J, was held during the week of September 30th through October 6th, with 39 trainees. Those included 17 staff from Steinway Child and Family Services, 2 from Fordham-Tremont Community Mental Health Center, and 3 from Long Island College Hospital and 17 volunteers. Those three facilities are referral sources for 32B-J EAP.

The third training, during the week of October 7th through 13th, was held at Fordham-Tremont Community Mental Health Center. The 16 trainees included 13 staff from Fordham-Tremont and 3 volunteers. The fourth training, also during the week of October 7th through 13th, was held at Long Island College Hospital. Nine trainees included 6 staff from the hospital and 3 volunteers.

Objective #3: Provide a course on compassion fatigue that will increase self-care for those mental health professionals and others who have provided services to the victims. The compassion fatigue course is designed to help the mental health professionals effectively manage their own stress so that they can continue to provide services.

Objective #4: Establish the headquarters of the New York Green Cross Project, establish the New York Green Cross Projects Chapter, and develop sufficient funding for at least one year.

Outcome: This objective was reached by establishing the headquarters of the New York Green Cross Project at the Host's building on the 23rd Floor. Two banners hung there during the mobilization. Fundraising is ongoing as are efforts to establish the local chapter in addition to two meetings in October. The American Red Cross (ARC) was providing mental health services at its Family Service Center, and routinely received requests from businesses for debriefing employees. The ARC contacted NYGCP to inquire if GCP would take ARC referrals. Additional GCP trauma workers were deployed to NYC to handle the increased need for trauma services. We anticipate that as routine and a sense of normality emerges in New York City, the need for the Chapter will increase. Trauma specialists recognize the difference between treating traumatic response versus treating mental health disorders, i.e., providing trauma management and coping skills rather than therapy. Collaboration and education in the mental health community are keys to ensuring that the appropriate treatment of traumatized individuals is delivered. The first organizational meeting was held October 1, 2001 at the Chinese United Methodist Church (69 Madison Street, New York City Chinatown District) from 4-6 PM.

In terms of other support secured for the New York Green Cross Project, the distinguished New York City law firm of Loeb & Loeb agreed to provide legal and other assistance for the coming months and particularly to help set up the NY Metro Chapter.

The generous pro bono assistance of Jet Blue, AirLifeLine, and other private aviators made it possible for GCP members to get in and out of the New York City metro area as quickly as possible.

Objective #5: Evaluate the Green Cross Projects deployment standard operating procedures and make needed improvements.

Outcome: An upcoming Annual Membership Meeting will discuss and evaluate the Green Cross Projects deployment standard operating procedures (SOP). A new SOP will emerge from these discussions and the After Action Report prepared by the second and third author. Modifications include use of Incident Command and deployment of compassion fatigue specialists. While a deployment structure had been informally adopted, the Incident Command System had not been used during prior deployments. For traumatologists trained in earlier courses, the Incident Command System was not part of their training. Consequently, only some team members were familiar with incident command. Those who were not familiar with incident command reported that the structure of incident command was too rigid. They had difficulty integrating the concepts of a chain of command system while working a catastrophic event. This created conflict that could have been avoided had the SOPs clearly stated the command structure. The addition of compassion fatigue specialists (CFS) as part of the team was a new concept, implemented for the first time during the September 11th response. The CFS primary responsibility was to ensure that GCP traumatologists providing services were able to manage the stresses of the catastrophic event. A secondary responsibility was to debrief/defuse the management staff. Although the concept of having CFS on the team was embraced by all, the reporting structure created boundary concerns for the CFS. Initially the compassion fatigue specialists were assigned to team leaders, and were directed to work only with members of their teams. When issues arose that included team leader concerns, boundary issues arose and the CFS was faced with a conflict of interest when trying to resolve. In future incidents, a deployment team CFS will report directly to the Incident Commander, and CFS for the trauma services teams will report to the Operations Manager.

Objective #6: Produce at least three reports of the lessons learned and publish them in *Traumatology*, the Green Cross Projects international electronic journal.

Outcome: The Editor of the Journal (the first author) sent a call for papers and reports from the GCP members who were involved in the mobilization and those who were active in providing assistance in some other ways.

During the thirty-day mobilization to reach the above objectives it became clear that there would be far more traumatized Host members and employees requesting trauma services. Moreover, the Red Cross established a good working relationship with area community-based organizations and mental health professionals to provide services to the traumatized, thus negating the need for establishing a local chapter of the GCP (Objective 4). However, there is ongoing interest and effort in establishing the chapter at the time this article was written.

To accomplish these objectives, Green Cross Project deployed a total of 36 Traumatologist volunteers from September 16 through October 17, 2001. The first week, September 16th through 22nd, 14 were deployed. The second week, September 23rd through 29th, 14 were deployed. The third week, September 30th through October 6th, 13 were deployed. The fourth week, October 7th through 13th, 11 were deployed. To maintain continuity of services, some team members were on site from one week to the next.

In an October 29, 2001 letter to the Green Cross Project's NYGCP project Incident Commander, Jim Norman, the President of the Host organization, Michael P. Fishman wrote:

It has been nearly a week since you left Local 32B-J. On October 19th we held a memorial service at St. Patrick's Cathedral for the 24 missing members. Over 4,000 members attended. In many ways, this memorial brought some closure to the first period of this terrible tragedy. But, I can say in all honesty that we would never have been able to get to this point without your efforts and the efforts of the Green Cross workers.

From the day you hit the ground, Green Cross brought an immeasurable degree of safety and calmness as we dealt with what was for many the most horrible and tragic event of their lives. Time after time, people would tell me how they were struggling to get by and because of some connection with one of the Green Cross volunteers, they were able to continue to assist our members and carry on in their own lives.

It is hard to imagine, in the beginning, that five weeks later we would begin to have some distance from this terrible event and be able to resume some semblance of a normal, although changed, life. For this we owe many thanks to you.

If there is anything we can do to help your organization, or you personally, please let me know. With many thanks.

Sincerely,
[signed]
Michael P. Fishman, President

DISCUSSION

Compared to the Oklahoma City bombing, the WTC attack was in a totally new category of traumatic events. The lessons learned in Oklahoma and in subsequent experiences were a necessary but not sufficient preparation for what the GCP had to face in New York City in 2001.

Unique Factors Associated with the WTC

1. Massiveness

The large numbers of those impacted in the immediate area, which included mental health practitioners, was extraordinary and unprecedented. As a result, GCP resources were strained. Unlike other programs, with traumatized folks trying to help traumatized folks, we were able to rotate fresh workers weekly and provide them with excellent resources during and following deployment. The first thirty days following an incident are ones in which the local providers need time to manage and begin healing their own traumatic reactions. By bringing in traumatologists from other states and countries, local resources are supported through the availability of those who can provided trauma assistance and, in the case of GCP deployment, provide desperately needed trauma recovery training. In addition, rotating workers provided an exposure cap to the amount of traumatic material to which the GCP workers would be exposed. This was critical in the management of compassion fatigue. Because the Host (Local 32B-J) had endorsed GCP as its resource for trauma management for staff and members, those needing trauma services were able to adapt to the new personnel when they arrived. (Note: Staggered arrivals allowed from the transition from one trauma worker to the next. At no time were 100% of the workers rotated out with a complete new team starting at the same time.)

War-Like Attack

Never before has any member worked a disaster that was an act of war. Although the Oklahoma City bombing was an act of terrorism, the perpetrator was caught and the potential for more such attacks seemed remote. Even following the first WTC bombing in 1993 the threat seemed manageable and the work of a fringe group. The 9-11 attack was especially troublesome because it seemed to serve as a prelude to other such attacks; that America was mobilizing to face such attacks; that it was the beginning, not an end, of something terrible. Future mobilizations must learn from these lessons and not attempt to apply without question lessons learned from natural disasters, accidents, and lesser crimes. While natural disasters, accidents and lesser crimes may include elements of horror, these incidents have a beginning and an end; they do not have international implications, and sons and daughters do not go off to war. The concept of "collateral damage" has entered our countries' consciousness. Our everyday lives are changed; and for some racial profiling has added another element of horror.

2. Air Quality

Although everyone who worked in or near ground zero were assured that the air was not toxic, that assurance was short lived. Soon, disaster workers and others working or living in lower Manhattan, including 32B-J workers, were feeling the symptoms, most notably persistent coughing. This was associated with a generalized anxiety about other health effects–both short and long-term. Several web sites were established to keep those who had such concerns informed. GCP Incident Command established a policy that its traumatologists were to stay out of the Ground Zero area. While the primary reason was to ensure that GCP workers were not exposed to traumatic stimuli that could inhibit their ability to provide services, a secondary benefit was to limit their exposure to "bad air." During wind shifts that would drift "bad air" northward the Host (Local 32B-J) provided masks to help minimize exposure. Future deployments need to be prepared for such health risks and make adequate preparation.

LESSONS LEARNED FROM GCP'S RESPONSE TO THE WTC DISASTER

At the November 10, 2001 GCP Annual Membership Meeting all of those who participated in the mobilization were honored with certificates. At that time these and other members shared their perspectives about what has happened and the lessons they had learned so far. Among other things that were shared are the following:

1. "Words Shape Beliefs Which Shape Behavior"

The primacy effect, long identified by social psychologists, applies to traumatized people whose initial beliefs often are hard to change. The belief that "God is punishing us," for example, was common among the survivors in New York with whom we worked. We found in this disaster, similar to others, that those beliefs galvanized by the traumatic event, operate in ways that validate the belief. Yet, for some, just hearing someone else articulate such a belief can also lead to actions. We made sure that training included the best ways to approach the traumatized who were just beginning to formulate their initial self-referencing statements vis-à-vis the trauma they had just survived. We were cautious about using such terms as "victims" and discussing symptoms they may experience for fear that it would increase the likelihood of acting and feeling like victims and becoming more symptomatic.

2. Most Traumatized Are Shaken But Not Broken

Were it not for the traumatic event, most of those we helped would not need our help. We expect them to spring back, be resilient, and emerge even stronger and better equipped to cope because of their experiences without experiencing disappointment or pity when they do not. We made sure that our training emphasized the need for trauma workers to approach the traumatized as those in crisis who are expected to get better.

3. Good Therapists Don't Equal Good Disaster Mental Health Specialists

A lesson noted often by Red Cross Disaster Mental Health Professionals (cf., Wee & Myers, 2002) is that Green Cross Project service providers must leave their traditional therapy skills and methods at home. GCP Training includes discussions of what *not* to do with the traumatized or those in crisis, in contrast to a client who is re-experiencing a memory of a trauma from many years ago. What works well for the latter does not necessarily work for the former.

4. Assess, Stabilize, and Refer (ASR)

Most people that experience trauma only need assessment and stabilization services. They are able then to get on with their life unless somehow they get the idea that they have some kind of *disorder*. Training must emphasize this, particularly for mental health professionals who are required to diagnose all clients and rarely work with healthy people. Well-adjusted individuals may, by virtue of their trauma experience, appear to be dysfunctional and indistinguishable from the typical mental health client. However, they are very different and need to be treated accordingly in order to avoid unintentionally conveying to them that they are more impaired than they are in actuality.

5. Incident Command Works Best in Disaster Response

Incident Command is the most useful approach in working mass casualty or mass population impacted by traumatic events. Training must do a better job of orienting mental health professionals about this approach. It is not taught in graduate programs and rarely discussed in Red Cross training. The Incident Command System (ICS) is used routinely in the public sector at the federal, state, county and municipal levels as a means to coordinate the effective use of all available resources during an emergency, regardless of the magnitude of that emergency (FEMA, 1998) (see: *http://www.fema.gov/emi/is195lst.htm*). The organizational structure consists of 5 major components (see Table 2).

The Incident Commander is responsible for management on scene. The GCP President (second author) served as the Incident Commander from September 11 through October 2, at which time the third author assumed command. Major responsibilities included management of personnel and equipment resources, maintaining accountability for tasks and safety, and establishing and maintaining an effective liaison with agencies and organizations.

The Operations Manager is directly responsible for ensuring that the mission of the organization is carried out. At Local 32B-J, the third author ensured that the mission–the delivery of trauma services to victims and training to local providers–was carried out.

TABLE 2. Incident Command Organizational Chart

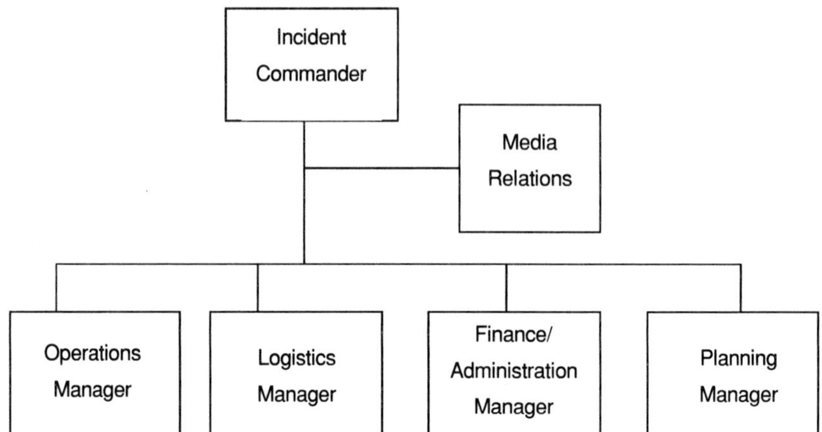

The Logistics Section is responsible for ensuring that facilities, services and materials are available to carry out the mission. During the September 11 response this included the coordination of transportation for all deployed personnel, coordination of hotel rooms, and the acquisition of appropriate equipment (e.g., telephones (land line and cell), computers, and hand held radios). Volunteers from the local area and 32B-J personnel fulfilled this role.

The Finance/Administration Section is responsible for tracking costs and making reimbursements. An example of this during the GCP September 11 response was documenting per diem disbursements, a role filled by Local 32B-J personnel.

The Planning Section is responsible for the collection, evaluation, dissemination, and use of information about the development of the incident and the status of resources. It may also include the development of an Incident Action Plan, which defines the response activities for a specified time frame. During the GCP response to September 11 a daily meeting was held which included the GCP Incident Commander, GCP Operations Manager, and Local 32B-J management. The agenda for the daily meetings was to summarize the activities of the day, evaluate if changes were necessary and brief staff of changes. During the first week of service delivery, meetings occurred more than once per day as needs among the staff and members emerged.

6. A Team Approach Is a Necessity for Effective Disaster Response

There must be trust in the plan and especially trust in the team approach. Working in teams is vital to a successful deployment. To be successful, a team must work with an agreed upon protocol and hierarchy. Effective training for disaster services must teach these procedures while emphasizing the importance of teamwork and maintaining team morale.

7. Compassion Fatigue Prevention Is Vital

Devoting at least one team member to the work of compassion fatigue prevention illustrates how the Green Cross is committed to self-care. The use of a self-care protocol is vital for effective functioning as a team and as team members. The benefits to those served are obvious. Self-care includes learning one's own personal signs and signals of increasing stress and knowing one's breaking point. Training should include simulations of the conditions found in extended mobilizations and insure that trainees develop their own plan for self-care and team care.

8. Retain a Calm Exterior

When working in a crisis setting it is vital to maintain a demeanor that represents stability, confidence, and warmth. This includes keeping one's voice low and soothing, speaking in short sentences and breathing deeply between sentences. Ask closed ended questions until stabilization occurs; then move into more opened ended questions. Training should emphasize the importance of asking permission to be present with someone and to never touch without invitation.

9. Stress Reactions Follow No Time Table

Often there is a delayed impact for some that experience trauma with no fixed time frame. People deal with these stressors when the time is right for them. For some, defenses against fully appreciating what they have survived may take years to subside although they do seem to eventually wear out.[2] Current traumatic events will often awaken memories of older traumas. Therefore, intervention needs to address those aspects of current and past trauma that are disturbing to each individual without pressing them to confront those that are not presently distressing to them. Training should reinforce this lesson and review the literature on delayed stress reactions.

10. Territoriality

In order to cope with these stressors, some exposed to trauma–both victims and workers–find that establishing and maintaining territories makes them feel safe. To do so provides a sense of control in an otherwise chaotic environment. Training should include information about group dynamics and how workers and victims may organize themselves in an effort to feel safer and more comfortable with negative consequences for others.

11. Emergency Professionals and Civilians Respond Differently

Civilians access and respond to their emotions much more readily than emergency professionals. This is due, in part, to the personality and experiences of these professionals, whose work often encompasses regular exposure to traumatic situations. In order to cope they often develop the strategy of trying to maintain a distance from their emotional responses. Also, emergency workers are most often men and their organizations tend to be male-oriented. Future training must include a discussion of these reactions, which are complicated and attribute to a number of dimensions beyond gender. All GCP mobilizations work with both emergency responders and therapists, who must quickly jell as a team in order to work effectively together. Training should include simulations that require practice in forming such teams to work well together.

12. Other Observations

First, it is critical to be able to access local professionals, particularly specialists in trauma, as soon as possible to both ask if there is a need for the GCP and (especially if there is) to recruit them to be part of the Project there ASAP so that they can take over once the crisis is over. Second, it is vital that there is good communication with and among GCP members who are or may be part of the mobilization. Web-based communication worked well for most but not all. Third, media relations are important in making sure that GCP maintains a positive reputation, that there is good public education about the challenges of the mobilization, and (most importantly) communicate with press releases to home town news organizations about their own people serving in the disaster with GCP. This latter element increases appreciation by the community for the worker and by the worker for the recognition.

A FINAL NOTE ABOUT THE SELF OF THE TRAUMA PRACTITIONER

We were *so* focused on the work at hand that the reality did not catch up with us fully until more than a month after the effort. Along the way we made sure that we wrote about the experience, talked about it, got needed rest and exercise, and did all the other things that we preach to others to do. Because each team had at least one person who specialized in compassion fatigue, everyone was constantly reminded to self-monitor stress levels and to actively practice self-care. Each training included elements of worker self care. There is an on-going assessment of the GCP members who were deployed and a progress report that emerged from the GCP at the Annual Membership Meeting late in 2001.

However, our experiences are consistent with Lahad's (2000) observation that it is vital that trauma workers understand the potential for experiencing the "fantasy of omnipotence" when delivering services and the enormous adaptive challenge following mobilization when the worker returns to life as usual.

On a more personal note, the first and second author, because they are marital partners, had the unusual opportunity to talk a great deal about what we each experienced as "fellow survivors" (Figley, 1985). Each in our own way has recognized the historic importance of the September 11th attack on Manhattan and that we experienced the extraordinary opportunity to apply our collective 45 years of professional experience through the New York Green Cross Project mobilization. The one thing that continued to invade our discussions–starting with our rushed humanitarian flight to New York from Tallahassee on September 16th–was the extraordinary loss of life and shattered dreams. It is as if we were aware of the huge tide of emotion held back by our mission of service.

Will any of us–New Yorkers, Americans, or any civilized human being–fully recognized what the world lost Tuesday morning, September 11, 2001? God help us all.

NOTES

1. The survey consisted of telephone interviews conducted under the direction of Princeton Survey Research Associates among a nationwide sample of 891 adults, 18 years of age or older, during the period October 10-14, 2001. For results based on the total sample, one can say with 95% confidence that the error attributable to sampling and other random effects is plus or minus 4 percentage points. For results based on October

10-11 (N = 400) or October 12-14 (N = 491), the sampling error is plus or minus 5.5 percentage points.

2. Just the week before the attack on the WTC one person, for example, who had worked with survivors of Oklahoma City bombing, had just then decided to address his "bombing stuff."

REFERENCES

Academy of Traumatology. (1999). Standards of practice for traumatologists. Author: Tallahassee, FL. Retrieved from *<www.greencross.org/Academy.html>*.

Doherty, G. W. (1999). Towards the next millennium: Disaster mental health–learning from the past and planning for the future. *Traumatology, 5*(2), Retrieved from *<http://www.fsu.edu/~trauma/a1v5i2.htm>*.

Figley, C. R. (1985). From victim to survivor: Social responsibility in the wake of catastrophe. In C.R. Figley (Ed.), *Trauma and its wake: The study and treatment of post-traumatic stress disorder* (pp. 398-416). New York: Brunner/Mazel.

Figley, C. R. (1998). The transition from registered to certified traumatologist. *Invited address to the Green Cross Projects Annual Conference.* Tampa, Florida.

Figley, C. R. (2002). Terrorism and traumatic stress. *Family Therapy Magazine, 1*(1), 10-12.

Figley, C. R. (in press). Theory-informed brief treatments. In C. R. Figley (Ed.), *Brief treatments for the traumatized sponsored by The Green Cross Foundation.* West Port, CT: Greenwood.

Fishman, M. (2001, November). Personal Communication.

Institute for Social Research. (2001). *How America responds (Part 1): Economic impact of terrorist attacks.* University of Michigan ISR. October.

Mooli, L. (2000). Darkness over the abyss: Supervising crisis intervention teams following disaster. *Traumatology, 6*(4), 273-294.

Pew Research Center for the People and the Press. (2001, October). America responds: Tracking survey, part I. Retrieved from *<http://www.people-press.org/midoct01que.htm>*.

Taylor, A. J. W. (1998). Observations from a cyclone stress/trauma assignment in the Cook Islands. *Traumatology, 4*(2). Retrieved from *<http://www.fsu.edu/~trauma/art3v4i1.html>*.

Wee, D., & Myers, D. (2002). Stress responses of mental health workers following disaster: The Oklahoma City bombing. In C. R. Figley (Ed.), *Brief treatments for the traumatized: Sponsored by The Green Cross Foundation,* 57-84. Westport, CT: Greenwood.

World Health Organization. (1997). *Management of mental disorders: Treatment protocol project.* (2nd.ed.). 2 vols. Darlinghurst, Sydney: World Health Organization Collaborating Centre for Mental Health & Substance Abuse.

Compassion Fatigue: A Crucible of Transformation

J. Eric Gentry

SUMMARY. This article explores the history, causes, treatments and prevention of compassion fatigue (the negative effects of helping others), contextualized for application to the trauma recovery efforts from the events of September 11, 2001. The author draws upon experience with development and implementation of the Accelerated Recovery Program for Compassion Fatigue, the Certified Compassion Fatigue Specialist Training, and the provision of treatment and training to hundreds of caregivers suffering from compassion fatigue symptoms. A model for understanding the multiple causes of compassion fatigue is presented, along with distillation of the active ingredients for effective treatment and prevention of its symptoms. Symptoms of compassion fatigue are conceptualized not only as disruptive and deleterious effects of caring for the traumatized, but also as a catalyst for positive change, transformation, maturation, and resiliency in the lives of these caregivers. Specific suggestions for compassion fatigue prevention and resiliency are reviewed.

J. Eric Gentry, PhD (cand.), MT, CAC, is affiliated with the International Trauma Institute, University of South Florida, 4202 East Fowler Avenue MHH116, Tampa, FL 33620 (e-mail: egentry@admin.usf.edu).

The author wishes to acknowledge support for this article from Anna Baranowsky, PhD, private practice, Toronto, Canada.

[Haworth co-indexing entry note]: "Compassion Fatigue: A Crucible of Transformation." Gentry, J. Eric. Co-published simultaneously in *Journal of Trauma Practice* (The Haworth Maltreatment & Trauma Press, an imprint of The Haworth Press, Inc.) Vol. 1, No. 3/4, 2002, pp. 37-61; and: *Trauma Practice in the Wake of September 11, 2001* (ed: Steven N. Gold, and Jan Faust) The Haworth Maltreatment & Trauma Press, an imprint of The Haworth Press, Inc., 2002, pp. 37-61. Single or multiple copies of this article are available for a fee from The Haworth Document Delivery Service [1-800-HAWORTH, 9:00 a.m. - 5:00 p.m. (EST). E-mail address: getinfo@haworthpressinc.com].

KEYWORDS. Treatment, prevention, compassion fatigue, helping others, trauma, recovery, September 11, Accelerated Recovery Program for Compassion Fatigue, Certified Compassion Fatigue Specialist Training, caregivers, training, resiliency

INTRODUCTION

On October 19, 2001 I co-facilitated a Critical Incident Stress Debriefing (CISD; Mitchell, 1995) in New York City for 12 mid-level retail managers who had been working two blocks from the World Trade Center on September 11, 2001. As this group navigated through the CISD and its cognitive-affective-cognitive "schwoop" (Norman, 2001), that hallmark of emergency psychology, one person began to describe the debris falling from the crumbling towers by saying, "In my mind I see chunks of concrete falling from the building but I know it was really people that I saw falling . . . jumping." As she spoke, I could not help myself from forming my own images of falling debris coalescing into anatomical features. Another participant reported that the worst part of September 11th for him was the emergence of recurrent intrusive images and nightmares. However, the intrusions he was experiencing were not of the horrors he saw in lower Manhattan; instead they were of tracer rounds from automatic rifles firing over his and his mother's head when he was a child fleeing Vietnam in 1975. As he described the spontaneous emergence of these memories, brought to consciousness for the first time in 26 years, I began to recall images from some of the thousands of combat trauma narratives I have heard from the hundreds of combat veterans that I have treated. I also began to feel some anxiety for the co-facilitator who was leading this debriefing, as this was his thirtieth straight day of providing trauma relief services in New York City and he was a Vietnam combat veteran.

While participating in this debriefing, I was acutely aware of my powerlessness to prevent the images, thoughts and feelings shared by the participants from finding their way into parallel associations in my own consciousness. Having spent the past five years studying and treating compassion fatigue, I knew that I was high risk for the development of secondary traumatic stress symptoms. For the next several weeks I experienced recurrent images and accompanying arousal from this and other experiences in New York. It was only after extensive support from colleagues and my work, as a client, with Eye Movement Desensitization & Reprocessing (EMDR) (Shapiro, 1995), that I was able to relegate these images and feelings from the encroaching present into the near-distant past.

Thousands of emergency service and mental health professionals have labored heroically to assist survivors of the events of 9/11/01. These service professionals have witnessed events and heard stories of incredible courage and resiliency in the course of providing assistance to the survivors. They have also been exposed to incidents and reports of life-shattering pain, terror, and loss. There is no doubt that there are great rewards associated with providing care and assistance to survivors of trauma; for those of us who have chosen traumatology as a professional path, there is no sweeter experience than witnessing a survivor emerge transformed and fortified from the dark jungle of posttraumatic symptoms. There is also, however, little doubt that serving these survivors exacts a toll that while minimal for some caregivers, can be devastating for others. As Viktor Frankl, one of the twentieth century's greatest traumatologists, simultaneously warns and encourages: "*That which is to give light must endure burning*" (Frankl, 1963).

This article explores the potential causes, prevention, and treatments of compassion fatigue (Figley, 1995), and the deleterious effects of helping the traumatized, as it relates to the tragedy of September 11, 2001. It is offered with the hope that it may help some of those dedicated to being of service to survivors in New York and across the nation to continue being givers of light, burning ever more brightly, and never burning out.

COMPASSION FATIGUE

The notion that working with people in pain extracts a significant cost from the caregiver is not new. Although the costs vary and have been lamented from time immemorial, anyone who has sat at the bedside of a seriously ill or recently bereaved loved one knows the toll involved in devoting singular attention to the needs of another suffering person. Only in recent years, however, has there been a substantial effort to examine the effects on the caregiver of bearing witness to the indescribable wounds inflicted by traumatic experiences. The exploration and examination of these effects evolved throughout the last century and comes to us from a wide variety of sources.

One of the first earliest references in the scientific literature regarding this cost of caring comes from Carl G. Jung in *The Psychology of Dementia Praecox* (Jung, 1907). In this text, Jung discusses the challenges of *countertransference*–the therapist's conscious and unconscious reactions to the patient in the therapeutic situation–and the particular countertransferential difficulties analysts encounter when working with psychotic patients. He boldly *prescribes* a treatment stance in which the therapist participates in the delusional fantasies and hallucinations *with* the patient. Nevertheless, he warns that this participation in the patient's darkly painful fantasy world of traumatic images has significant deleterious effects for the therapist, especially the neophyte and/or the therapist who has not resolved his/her own developmental and traumatic issues (Sedgewick, 1995).

The study of countertransference produced the first writings in the field of psychotherapy that systematically explored the effects of psychotherapy upon the therapist (Haley, 1974; Danieli, 1982; Lindy, 1988; Wilson & Lindy, 1994; Karakashian, 1994; Pearlman & Saakvitne, 1995). Recent texts have suggested that therapists sometimes experience countertransference reactions that imitate the symptoms of their clients (Herman, 1992; Pearlman & Saakvitne, 1995). For instance, when working with survivors of traumatic experiences, authors have reported countertransference phenomena that mimic the symptoms of posttraumatic stress disorder (PTSD) (Lindy, 1988; Wilson & Lindy, 1994; Pearlman & Saakvitne, 1995).

Business and industry, with their progressive focus upon productivity in the last half of the twentieth century, have provided us with the concept of burnout (Fruedenberger, 1974; Maslach, 1976) to describe the deleterious effects the environmental demands of the workplace have on the worker. Burnout, or "the syndrome of emotional exhaustion, depersonalization, and reduced personal accomplishment" (Maslach, 1976), has been used to describe the chronic effects that psychotherapists suffer as a result of interactions with their clients and/or the demands of their workplace (Freudenberger, 1974; Cherniss, 1980; Farber, 1983; Sussman, 1992; Grosch & Olsen, 1995; Maslach & Goldberg, 1998). Research has shown that therapists are particularly vulnerable to burnout because of personal isolation, ambiguous successes and the emotional drain of remaining empathetic (McCann & Pearlman, 1990). Moreover, burnout not only is psychologically debilitating to therapists, but also impairs the therapist's capacity to deliver competent mental health services (Farber, 1983). The literature on burnout, with its twenty-five year history, thoroughly describes the phenomena and prescribes preventive and treatment interventions for helping professionals.

The study of the effects of trauma has also promoted a better undertanding of the negative effects of helping. Psychological reactions to trauma have been described over the past one hundred and fifty years by various names such as "shell shock," "combat neurosis," "railroad spine," and "combat fatigue" (Shalev, Bonne, & Eth, 1996). However, not until 1980 was the latest designation for these reactions, posttraumatic stress disorder (PTSD), formally recognized as an anxiety disorder in the *Diagnostic and Statistical Manual of Mental Disorders-III* (DSM-III) (American Psychiatric Association, 1980; Matsakis, 1994). Since that time, research into posttraumatic stress has grown at an exponential rate (Figley, 1995; Wilson & Lindy, 1994) and the field of traumatology has been established with two of its own journals, several professional organizations, and unique professional identity (Figley, 1988; Bloom, 1999; Gold & Faust, 2001).

As therapists are increasingly called upon to assist survivors of violent crime, natural disasters, childhood abuse, torture, acts of genocide, political persecution, war, and now terrorism (Sexton, 1999), discussion regarding the reactions of therapists and other helpers to working with trauma survivors has recently emerged in the traumatology literature (Figley, 1983, 1995; Danieli, 1988; McCann & Pearlman, 1990; Pearlman & Saakvitne, 1995; Stamm, 1995). Professionals who listen to reports of trauma, horror, human cruelty and extreme loss can become overwhelmed and may begin to experience feelings of fear, pain and suffering similar to that of their clients. They may also experience PTSD symptoms similar to their clients, such as intrusive thoughts, nightmares, avoidance and arousal, as well as changes in their relationships to their selves, their families, friends and communities (Figley, 1995; McCann & Pearlman, 1990, Salston, 1999). Therefore, they may themselves come to need assistance to cope with the effects of listening to others' traumatic experiences (Figley, 1995; Pearlman & Saakvitne, 1995; Saakvitne, 1996; Gentry, Baranowsky & Dunning, 1997, in press).

While the empirical literature has been slow to develop in this area, there is an emerging body of scientific publications that attempts to identify and define the traumatization of helpers through their efforts of helping. Pearlman and Saakvitne (1995), Figley (1995), and Stamm (1995) all authored and/or edited texts that explored this phenomenon among helping professionals during the same pivotal year. The terms "vicarious traumatization" (McCann & Pearlman, 1990; Pearlman & Saakvitne, 1995), "secondary traumatic stress" (Figley, 1987; Stamm, 1995) and "compassion fatigue" (Figley, 1995) have all become cornerstones in the vernacular of describing the deleterious effects that helpers suffer when working with trauma survivors.

Vicarious traumatization (McCann & Pearlman, 1990) refers to the transmission of traumatic stress through observation and/or hearing others' stories of traumatic events and the resultant shift/distortions that occur in the caregiver's perceptual and meaning systems. Secondary traumatic stress occurs when one is exposed to extreme events directly experienced by another and becomes overwhelmed by this secondary exposure to trauma (Figley & Kleber, 1995). Several theories have been offered but none has been able to conclusively demonstrate the mechanism that accounts for the transmission of traumatic stress from one individual to another. It has been hypothesized that the caregiver's level of empathy with the traumatized individual plays a significant role in this transmission (Figley, 1995) and some budding empirical data to support this hypothesis (Salston, 2000).

Figley (1995) also proposes that the combined effects of the caregiver's continuous visualizing of clients' traumatic images added to the effects of burnout can create a condition progressively debilitating the caregiver that he has called "compassion stress." This construct holds that exposure to clients' stories of traumatization can produce a form of posttraumatic stress disorder in which Criterion A, or "the event" criterion, is met through listening to, instead of the *in vivo* experiencing of, a traumatic event. The symptoms of compassion fatigue, divided into categories of intrusive, avoidance, and arousal symptoms, are summarized in Table 1.

As a result of our work with hundreds of caregivers suffering the effects of compassion fatigue, we have augmented Figley's (1995) definition to include pre-existing and/or concomitant primary posttraumatic stress and its symptoms. Many caregivers, especially those providing on-site services, will have had first-hand exposure to the traumatic event(s) to which they are responding (Pole et al., 2001; Marmar et al., 1999). For many, these symptoms of PTSD will have a delayed onset and not become manifest until some time later. We have also found that many caregivers enter the service field with a host of traumatic experiences in their developmental past (Gentry, 1999). There may have been no symptoms associated with these events, or the symptoms related to them may have remained sub-clinical. However, we have observed that as these caregivers begin to encounter the traumatic material presented by clients, many of them begin to develop clinical PTSD symptoms associated with their previously "benign" historical experiences. In our efforts to treat compassion fatigue, we have concluded that it is often necessary to successfully address and resolve primary traumatic stress before addressing any issues of secondary traumatic stress and/or burnout. Additionally, we have discerned an interactive, or synergistic, effect among primary traumatic stress, secondary traumatic stress, and burnout symptoms in the life of an afflicted caregiver. Experiencing symptoms from any one of these three sources appears to diminish resiliency and lower thresholds for the adverse impact of the other two. This seems to lead to a rapid onset of se-

TABLE 1. Comparison Fatigue Symptoms

Intrusive Symptoms
• Thoughts and images associated with client's traumatic experiences • Obsessive and compulsive desire to help certain clients • Client/work issues encroaching upon personal time • Inability to "let go" of work-related matters • Perception of survivors as fragile and needing the assistance of caregiver ("savior") • Thoughts and feelings of inadequacy as a caregiver • Sense of entitlement or special-ness • Perception of the world in terms of victims and perpetrators • Personal activities interrupted by work-related issues
Avoidance Symptoms
• Silencing Response (avoiding hearing/witnessing client's traumatic material) • Loss of enjoyment in activities/cessation of self care activities • Loss of energy • Loss of hope/sense of dread working with certain clients • Loss of sense of competence/potency • Isolation • Secretive self-medication/addiction (alcohol, drugs, work, sex, food, spending, etc.) • Relational dysfunction
Arousal Symptoms
• Increased anxiety • Impulsivity/reactivity • Increased perception of demand/threat (in both job and environment) • Increased frustration/anger • Sleep disturbance • Difficulty concentrating • Change in weight/appetite • Somatic symptoms

vere symptoms that can become extremely debilitating to the caregiver within a very short period of time (see Table 2).

ACCELERATED RECOVERY PROGRAM FOR COMPASSION FATIGUE

In 1997, two Green Cross Scholars and one doctoral student under the direction and supervision of Charles Figley at Florida State University developed the Accelerated Recovery Program for Compassion Fatigue (Gentry, Baranowsky & Dunning, 1997, in press; Gentry & Baranowsky, 1998, 1999, 1999a, 1999b). This five-session manualized and copyrighted protocol[1] was designed to address the symptoms of secondary traumatic stress and burnout, or compassion fatigue, in caregivers. Phase

TABLE 2. Compassion Fatigue Model

The Gentry/Baranowsky (1997) Model of Compassion Fatigue
PRIMARY TRAUMATIC STRESS
+/x (synergistic effect)
SECONDARY TRAUMATIC STRESS
+/x (synergistic effect)
BURNOUT
COMPASSION FATIGUE

one clinical trials with this protocol was completed with the developers and seven volunteers from various disciplines and backgrounds who had experience working with trauma survivors.[2] The qualitative data obtained from these initial volunteers were utilized to create the final version of the protocol. Each of these participants reported clinically significant lessening of compassion fatigue symptoms with one exception.[3]

The Accelerated Recovery Program (ARP) was presented in the fall of 1997 at the International Society for Traumatic Stress Studies (ISTSS) in Montreal, Canada. In attendance at this presentation was an official with the Federal Bureau of Investigation who requested that the developers provide training to his staff, and, subsequent to this training, the Accelerated Recovery Program was adopted for use in this agency (McNally, 1998, personal communication). As a result of contacts made through the FBI, twelve professional helpers who have provided on-going assistance to the survivors of the bombing of the Murrah Building in Oklahoma City requested treatment for their compassion fatigue symptoms through the Traumatology Institute at Florida State University. The ARP provided statistically and clinically significant successful treatment for each of these professionals (Gentry, 2000). Subsequent presentations on the ARP at ISTSS meetings in 1998, 1999, and the development of the Certified Compassion Fatigue Specialist Training (CCFST) have lead to the successful treatment of hundreds of caregivers with compassion fatigue symptoms through the Accelerated Recovery Program all over the world.

CERTIFIED COMPASSION FATIGUE SPECIALIST TRAINING: TRAINING-AS-TREATMENT

In late 1998, Gentry and Baranowsky, two of the developers of the Accelerated Recovery Program, were approached by the Traumatology Institute at Florida State University to create a training program for helping professionals interested in developing expertise in treating compassion fatigue. Through initial consultations, it was decided that the training would be designed around the ARP Model and that the participants would receive training on the implementation of the five sessions of this protocol. In addition, the training was designed to provide the participants with an in-depth understanding of the etiology, phenomenology and treatment/prevention of compassion fatigue, including secondary traumatic stress and burnout. The participants of this training would be certified by Florida State University's Traumatology Institute as Compassion Fatigue Specialists and authorized to implement the Accelerated Recovery Program for other caregivers suffering from compassion fatigue symptoms.

In their design of the program, the developers decided that the participants should receive first-hand experiential training for each of the interventions used in the Accelerated Recovery Program. With this in mind, the 17-hour training was developed and manualized (Gentry & Baranowsky, 1998, 1999a) with a focus upon the experiential components of the ARP. This phase in development of the Certified Compassion Fatigue Specialist Training (CCFST) was the first conceptualization of the "*training-as-treatment*" (Gentry, 2000) model for addressing the participants' symptoms of compassion fatigue. The rationale was that since the interventions of the ARP were effective working with individuals, the interventions would also be effective with these symptoms, albeit to a lesser degree, with the participants of the training.

It was then decided that the collection of baseline and outcome data would be conducted from the first training that was implemented in January of 1999. Baseline and post-training scores from compassion fatigue, compassion satisfaction and burnout subscales of the Compassion Satisfaction/Fatigue Self-Test (Figley, 1995; Figley & Stamm, 1996) were collected. Data were analyzed for 166 participants who successfully completed the CCFS Training between January 1999 and January 2001 (Gentry, 2000). The protocol demonstrated clinically and statically significant results ($p < .001$) when pre-training and post-training scores on the compassion fatigue, compassion satisfaction and burnout subscales of the Compassion Satisfaction/Fatigue Self-Test (Figley & Stamm, 1996) were compared.

TREATMENT AND PREVENTION: ACTIVE INGREDIENTS

It has been demonstrated that the potential to develop negative symptoms associated with our work in providing services to trauma survivors, especially the symptoms of secondary traumatic stress, increases as our exposure to their traumatic material increases (McCann & Pearlman, 1990; Salston, 2000). We believe that no one who chooses to work with trauma survivors is immune to the potential deleterious effects of this work. However, in our work with providing effective treatment to hundreds of caregivers with compassion fatigue symptoms, either individually through the ARP or in CCFS training groups, we have identified some enduring principles, techniques, and ingredients that seem to consistently lead to these positive treatment outcomes and enhanced resiliency.

Intentionality

Initiation of effective resolution of compassion fatigue symptoms requires specific recognition and acceptance of the symptoms and their causes by the caregiver, along with a decision to address and resolve these symptoms. Many caregivers who experience symptoms of compassion fatigue will attempt to ignore their distress until a threshold of discomfort is reached. For many caregivers this may mean that they are unable to perform their jobs as well as they once did or as well as they would like due to the symptoms they are experiencing. For others, it may entail the progressive debilitation associated with somatic symptoms or the embarrassment and pain associated with secretive self-destructive comfort-seeking behaviors. Whatever the impetus, we have found that successful amelioration of compassion fatigue symptoms requires that the caregiver intentionally acknowledge and address, rather than avoid, these symptoms and their causes. Additionally, we have found the use of goal-setting and the development of a personal/professional mission statement to be invaluable in moving away from the reactivity associated with the victimization of compassion fatigue and toward the resiliency and intentionality of mature caregiving.

Connection

One of the ways trauma seems to affect us all, caregivers included, is to leave us with a sense of disconnected isolation. A common thread we have found with sufferers of compassion fatigue symptoms has been the progressive loss in their sense of connection and community. Many caregivers become increasingly isolatory as their symptoms intensify. Fear of being perceived as weak, impaired, or incompetent by peers and clients, along with time constraints and loss of interest, have all been cited by caregivers suffering from compassion fatigue as reasons for diminished intimate and collegial connection. The development and maintenance of healthy relationships, which the caregiver uses for both support and to share/dilute the images and stories associated with secondary traumatic stress, may become a powerful mitigating factor in resolving and preventing compassion fatigue symptoms. Often the bridge for this connection is established in the peer-to-peer offering of the ARP, during which the facilitator works intentionally to develop a strong relationship with the caregiver suffering compassion fatigue symptoms. In the CCFST, we facilitate exercises specifically designed to dismantle interpersonal barriers and enhance self-disclosure. It seems that it is through these relational connections that the caregivers suffering compassion fatigue are able to gain insight and understanding that their symptoms are not an indication of some pathological weakness or disease, but are instead natural consequences of providing care for traumatized individuals. In addition, with the enhanced self-acceptance attained through self-disclosure with and by empathetic and understanding peers, caregivers are able to begin to see their symptoms as indicators of the developmental changes needed in both their self-care and caregiving practices. We have seen that a warm, supportive environment in which caregivers are able to discuss intrusive traumatic material, difficult clients, symptoms, fears, shame, and secrets with peers to be one of the most critical ingredients in the resolution and continued prevention of compassion fatigue.

Anxiety Management/Self-Soothing

It is our belief that providing caregiving services while experiencing intense anxiety is one of the primary means by which compassion fatigue symptoms are contracted and exacerbated. Alternately stated, to the degree that a caregiver is able to remain non-anxious (relaxed pelvic floor muscles), we believe, s/he will maintain resistance to the development of symptoms of compassion fatigue. The ability to self-regulate and soothe anxiety and stress is thought to be a hallmark of maturity. The mastery of these skills comes only with years of practice. However, if we fail to develop the capacity for self-regulation, if we are unable to internally attenuate our own levels of arousal, then we are susceptible to perceiving as threats those people, objects, and situations to which we respond with anxiety–believing that benign people, objects and situations are dangerous. As one very insightful and astute psychologist who was a participant in the CCFST stated: "Maybe the symptoms of compassion fatigue are a good thing, they force us to become stronger." It does seem to be true that those caregivers with well-developed self-regulation skills who do not resort to self-destructive and addictive comfort-seeking behaviors are unlikely to suffer symptoms of compassion fatigue.

In both the ARP and the CCFST, we work rigorously with participant caregivers to help them develop self-management plans that will assist them in achieving and maintaining an *in vivo* non-anxious presence. This non-anxious presence extends far beyond a calm outward appearance. Instead, it entails the ability to maintain a level of relaxed mindfulness and comfort in one's own body. This ability to remain non-anxious when confronted with the pain, horror, loss, and powerlessness associated with the traumatic experiences in the lives of clients, of having the capacity to calmly "bear witness," remains a key ingredient in the resolution and prevention of compassion fatigue symptoms.

Self-Care

Closely associated with self-management is the concept of self-care, or the ability to refill and refuel oneself in healthy ways. It is quite common for caregivers to find themselves anxious during and after working with severely traumatized individuals. Instead of developing a system of healthy practices for resolving this anxiety–such as sharing with colleagues, exercise, meditation, nutrition, and spirituality–many caregivers find themselves redoubling their work efforts. Frequently this constricting cycle of working harder in an attempt to feel better creates a distorted sense of entitlement that can lead to a breach of personal and professional boundaries. We have worked with many caregivers who have reported falling prey to compulsive behaviors such as overeating, overspending, or alcohol/drug abuse in an effort to soothe the anxiety they feel from the perceived demands of their work. Others with whom we have worked have self-consciously admitted to breaching professional boundaries and ethics when at the low point in this cycle, distortedly believing that they "deserve" this "special" treatment or reward.

Meta-analyses of psychotherapy outcomes consistently point toward the quality of the relationship between therapist and client as the single most important ingredient in positive outcomes (Bergin & Garfield, 1994). The integrity and quality of this relationship is contingent upon the therapist's maintenance of his/her instrument, the "self of the therapist." When caregivers fail to maintain a life that is rich with meaning and gratification outside the professional arena, then they often look to work as the sole source of these commodities. In this scenario, caregivers interact with their clients from a stance of depletion and need. It is completely understandable that this orientation would produce symptoms in caregivers. Conversely, professionals who responsibly pursue and acquire this sense of aliveness outside the closed system of their professional role are able to engage in work with traumatized individuals while sharing their own fullness, meaning, and joy. The cycle of depletion by our work and intentionally refilling ourselves in our lives outside of work, often on a daily basis, may have been what Frankl meant when he challenged us to "endure burning."

One of the most important aspects of this category of self-care that we have found in our work with caregivers has been the development and maintenance of a regular exercise regimen. No other single behavior seems to be as important than regular aerobic and anaerobic activity. In addition to exercise, good nutrition, artistic expression/discipline (e.g., piano lessons and composition, dance classes and choreography, structural planning and building), meditation/mindfulness, outdoor recreation, and spirituality all seem to be important ingredients to a good self-care plan.

We have found a few caregivers with compassion fatigue symptoms that seemed to be at least partially caused by working beyond their level of skill. Working with traumatized individuals, families, and communities is a highly skilled activity that demands many years of training in many different areas before one gains a sense of mastery. Trying to shortcut this process by prematurely working with trauma survivors without adequate training and supervision can very easily overwhelm even seasoned clinicians, much less neophytes. While empirical research has not yet addressed the effects of working beyond levels of competency or of providing services while impaired with stress symptoms has upon the care provider, especially in contexts of mass casualties like we have witnessed in New York City, we believe that these factors contribute significantly to the frequency, duration and intensity of compassion fatigue symptoms.

Sometimes training in the area of treating trauma, especially experiential trainings such as EMDR (Shapiro, 1995) or TIR (French & Harris, 1998), can have a powerful ameliorative effect upon compassion fatigue, bringing a sense of empowerment to a caregiver who was previously overwhelmed. The caveat here is that there exists some danger that an overwhelmed therapist who has been recently trained in one of these powerful techniques may emerge from the training with an inflated sense of skill and potency. Newly empowered, this therapist may be tempted to practice even further beyond their level of competence and skill. This scenario highlights the importance of good professional supervision during the developmental phases of a traumatologist's career. In addition, many therapists working with trauma survivors have found it helpful to receive periodic "check ups" with a trusted professional or peer supervisor. This is especially true during and immediately following deployment in a disaster or critical incident situation. These professional and peer supervisory relationships can serve as excellent opportunities to share, and therefore dilute the effects, of the artifacts of secondary traumatic stress that may have been collected while in service to trauma survivors. Professional supervision is also reported to have an overall ameliorative effect upon compassion fatigue symptoms (Pearlman, 1995; Catherall, 1995).

Every caregiver's self-care needs are different. Some will need to remain vigilant in the monitoring and execution of their self-care plan, while others will, seemingly, be able to maintain resiliency with minimal effort. However, we strongly urge the caregiver who specializes in working with trauma and trauma survivors to develop a comprehensive self-care plan that addresses and meets the caregiver's individual needs for each of the areas discussed in this article. With this self-care plan in place, the caregiver can now practice with the assurance that they are maximizing resiliency toward and prevention of the symptoms of compassion fatigue that is akin to the protection of wearing a seatbelt while driving an automobile.

It should be noted that those care providers responding on-site to crisis situations, such as those caused by the events of September 11, may be limited in their ability to employ habitual self-care activities. They may not have access to gymnasiums or exercise facilities, nutritious food and water may be scarce for a period of time, and it is doubtful that care providers deployed in situations of mass destruction will have access to their traditional support network. While most trauma responders are a hardy and resilient breed, we simply cannot sustain the rigors of this depleting and intensive work without intentional concern for our own health and welfare. Making best use of available resources to establish respite and sanctuary for ourselves, even in the most abject of circumstances, can have an enormous effect in minimizing our symptoms and maximizing our sustained effectiveness. Many responders have reported acts of kindness as simple as the gift of a bottle of water, a pat on the back, or an opportunity to share a meal with another responder as having a powerfully positive impact upon their morale and energy during these difficult times.

Narrative

Many researchers and writers have identified the creation of a chronological verbal and/or graphic narrative as an important ingredient in the healing of traumatic stress, especially intrusive symptoms (Tinnin, 1994; van der Kolk, 1996; Foa et al., 1999). We have found that a creation of a time-line narrative of a caregiving career that identifies the experiences and the clients from which the caregiver developed primary and secondary traumatic stress is invaluable in the resolution of compassion fatigue symptoms, especially those associated with secondary traumatic stress. In the ARP, we instruct the participant/caregiver to "tell your story . . . from the beginning–the first experiences in your life that led you toward caregiving–to the present." We use a video camera to record this narrative and ask the caregiver to watch it later that same day, taking care to identify the experiences that have led to any primary and secondary traumatic stress (intrusive symptoms) by constructing a graphic time-line. In the CCFST, we utilize dyads in which two participants each take a one-hour block of time to verbalize their narrative while the other practices non-anxious "bearing witness" of this narrative.

Desensitization and Reprocessing

With the narrative completed and the identification of historical experiences that are encroaching upon present-day consciousness and functioning in the form of primary and secondary traumatic stress, the caregiver is now ready to resolve these memories. In the ARP, we have utilized Eye Movement Dissociation and Reprocessing (Shapiro, 1989, 1995) as the method-of-choice for this work. In the CCFST, we utilize a hybridized version of a Neuro-Linguistic Programming Anchoring Technique (Baranowsky & Gentry, 1998). Any method that simultaneously employs exposure and relaxation (i.e., reciprocal inhibition) is appropriate for this important cornerstone of treatment. We have had success utilizing Traumatic Incident Reduction (French & Harris, 2000), the anamnesis procedure from the Trauma Recovery Institute (TRI) Method (Tinnin, 1994), or many of the techniques from Cognitive-Behavioral Therapy (Foa & Meadows, 1997; Follette, Ruzek, & Abueg, 1998; Rothbaum, Meadows, Resick, & Foy, 2000). With the successful desensitization and reprocessing of the caregiver's primary and secondary traumatic stress, and the cessation of intrusive symptoms, often comes a concomitant sense of rebirth, joy, and transformation. This important step and ingredient in the treatment of compassion fatigue should not be minimized or overlooked.

In our work with the responders of the Oklahoma City bombing, none reported experiencing intrusive symptoms of secondary and/or primary traumatic stress until several days, weeks, months, and sometimes years after their work at the site. From personal communication with an Incident Commander for a team of mental health responders who worked with over 2700 victims in New York City the first month after the attacks (Norman, 2002), he indicated that at least one Certified Compassion Fatigue Specialist was available to provide daily debriefing services for every 10 responders. He further indicated that if a responder began to report symptoms or show signs of significant traumatic stress, they were provided with acute stabilization services by the team and arrangements were made for transportation back home with a referral to a mental health practitioner in the worker's home town. With the intense demands of critical incident work and the paramount importance of worker safety, attempts of desensitization and reprocessing care provider's primary and secondary traumatic stress while on-site seems counterproductive as it draws from the often already depleted resources of the intervention team. For this reason, it is recommended that the worker engage in resolving the effects of accumulated traumatic memories only after safely returning to the existing resources and support offered by their family, friends, churches/synagogues, and health care professionals in their hometown.

Self-Supervision

This aspect of treatment is focused upon the correction of distorted and coercive cognitive styles. Distorted thinking may be developmental (i.e., existent prior to a caregiver's career), or may have been developed in response to primary and secondary traumatic stress later in life. Whatever the cause, we have found that once a caregiver contracts the negative symptoms of compassion fatigue, these symptoms will not fully resolve until distorted beliefs about self and the world are in the process of correction. This is especially true for the ways in which we supervise and motivate ourselves. Caregivers recovering from the symptoms of compassion fatigue will need to soften their critical and coercive self-talk and shift their motivational styles toward more self-accepting and affirming language and tone if they wish to resolve their compassion fatigue symptoms. For many this is a difficult, tedious, and painstaking breaking-of-bad-habits process than can take years to complete. In the ARP and the CCFST, we have employed an elegant and powerful technique called "video-dialogue" (Holmes & Tinnin, 1996) that accelerates this process significantly. This technique, adapted for use with the ARP, challenges the participant to write a letter to themselves from the perspective of the "Great Supervisor," lavishing upon themselves all the praise, support, and validation that they wish from others. They are then requested to read this letter into the eye of the camera. While watching back the videotape of this letter, the caregiver is asked to "pay attention to any negative or critical thought that thwarts your acceptance of this praise." Then, s/he is instructed to give these critical and negative thoughts a "voice," as these negative thoughts are articulated into the video camera, directed at the caregiver. This back-and-forth argument between the "self" and the "critical voice" of the caregiver continues on videotape until both "sides" begin to see the utility in both perspectives. With this completed, polarities relax, self-criticism softens, and integration is facilitated.

While this technique is powerfully evocative and can rapidly transform self-critical thinking styles, the Cognitive Therapy "triple column technique" (Burns, 1980), that helps identify particular cognitive distortions and challenges a client to rewrite these negative thoughts into ones that are more adaptive and satisfying, will also work well for this task. Additionally, as caregivers suffering from compassion fatigue symptoms develop some mastery in resolving these internal polarities with themselves, they are challenged to identify and resolve polarities with significant others. Individuals traumatized from either primary or secondary sources who are able to "un-freeze" themselves from their polarities, resentments, conflicts, and cut-offs will be rewarded with less anxiety, a heightened sense of comfort inside their own skin, and a greater sense of freedom from the past to pursue their mission of the present and future.

THE CRUCIBLE OF TRANSFORMATION

Our initial intent in developing the ARP was to simply gather a collection of powerful techniques and experiences that would rapidly ameliorate the suffering from symptoms of compassion fatigue in the lives of caregivers so that they would be able to return to their lives and their work refreshed and renewed. However, as we embarked upon yoking ourselves with the formidable task of sitting across from our peers who were suffering with these symptoms, many of whom were demoralized, hopeless, and desperate, we began to understand that recovery from compassion fatigue required significant changes in the foundational beliefs and lifestyles of the caregiver. As we navigated through the five sessions of the ARP with these suffering professionals we found that most underwent a significant transformation in the way in which they perceived their work and, ultimately, themselves.

Drawing from the work of David Schnarch (1991), who works with enmeshed couples to develop self-validated intimacy and achieve sexual potentials in their marriages, we began to see that many caregivers exhibited a similar form of enmeshment with their *careers*. We found that many of those suffering with compassion fatigue symptoms maintained an other-validated stance in their caregiving work–they were compelled to gain approval and feelings of worth from their clients, supervisors, and peers. In beginning to explore the developmental histories of many of the caregivers with whom we have worked, we found that many carried into their adult lives, and careers, unresolved attachment and developmental issues. For the caregiver who operates from an other-validated stance, clients, supervisors, and peers all represent potential threats when approval is withheld. These perceptions of danger and threat by the caregiver, which are enhanced by secondary traumatic stress contracted in work with trauma survivors, often lead to increased anxiety, feelings of victimization, and a sense of overwhelming powerlessness. As the caregiver is able to evolve toward a more self-validated stance and become more grounded in the non-anxious present, these symptoms begin to permanently dissipate. Pearlman and Saakvitne (1995) urge therapists to "find self-worth that is not based on their professional achievements. It is essential to develop and nurture spiritual lives outside our work" (p. 396). While we have found no existing empirical data in this ripe area of study, from a treatment perspective we began to see how the symptoms of compassion fatigue make sense in the lives of many professional caregivers, urging them towards maturation.

Instead of viewing the symptoms of compassion fatigue as a pathological condition that requires some external treatment agent or techniques for resolution, we began to see these symptoms as indicators of the need for the professional caregiver to continue his/her development into matured caregiving and self-care styles and practices. From this perspective the symptoms of compassion fatigue can be interpreted as *messages* from what is right, good, and strong within us, rather than indicators of shameful weaknesses, defects, or sickness.

Through our continued working with caregivers suffering the effects of secondary traumatic stress and burnout, we have been able to distill two primary principles of treatment and prevention that lead to a rapid resolution of symptoms and sustained resilience from future symptoms. These two important principles, which have become the underlying goals for our work in the area of compassion fatigue, are: (1) the development and maintenance of intentionality, through a non-anxious presence, in both personal and professional spheres of life, and (2) the development and maintenance of self-validation, especially self-validated caregiving. We have found, in our own practices and with the caregivers that we have treated, that when these principles are followed not only do negative symptoms diminish, but also quality of life is significantly enhanced and refreshed as new perspectives and horizons begin to open (see Table 3).

CONCLUSION

There is little doubt that the extensive efforts being devoted to assisting those affected by the events of September 11, 2001 will have far-reaching influence on the healing of survivors in New York, the people of our nation, and the people of the world. For the first time in the history of our planet, we are beginning to accumulate sufficient knowledge, skills, and resources to facilitate recovery and healing from events such as these. This is not to say that we will not all have painful losses to accommodate or indelible psychological scars–but we will recover. It is a humbling experience to participate, on any level, in this healing.

From our experience with the emergency service workers and professional caregivers who served the survivors of the Murrah building bombing on Oklahoma City since 1995, we also know that there will be casualties in this effort. Many kind and good-hearted emergency service professionals, caregivers, friends, and family members who have witnessed the pain, grief, and terror in their service to survivors will themselves end up wrestling with encroaching intrusive images, thoughts, and feelings from these interactions in the weeks, months, and years ahead.

Compassion fatigue is an area of study that is in its infancy. Therefore, very little empirical research has yet been published in this important area. However, the empirical research that does exist and the stories of hundreds of suffering caregivers provides us with evidence that compassion fatigue, and its painful symptoms, are a very real phenomenon (Deutch, 1984; Pearlman & McCann, 1990; Follette et al., 1994; Schauben & Frazier, 1995; Cerney , 1995; Salston, 2000). These symptoms carry with them the potential to disrupt, dissolve, and destroy careers, families, and even lives (many of us grieve the loss of at least one

TABLE 3. Suggestions for Compassion Fatigue Prevention and Resiliency

If you or someone you know is experiencing symptoms of compassion fatigue, the following suggestions may be helpful. Please check with your family physician to assure that there are no physical illnesses associated with these symptoms first.

- Become more informed. Read Figley (1995), Stamm (1995) and/or Pearlman and Saakvitne (1995) to learn more about the phenomena of compassion fatigue, vicarious traumatization, and secondary traumatic stress. One book that is especially helpful is *Transforming The Pain: A Workbook on Vicarious Traumatization* by Saakvitne and Pearlman (1996).
- Join a Traumatic Stress Study Group. A weekly, bi-weekly or monthly meeting of trauma practitioners can become an excellent sanctuary in which the caregiver can both share (therefore diluting) traumatic stories as well as receive support. Check with the ISTSS (*www.istss.org*) for a group that may meet in your area or start one of your own. There are several on-line support resources also. You can find some of these resources through the excellent David Balwin's Trauma Pages (*http://www.trauma-pages.com*) in the "Resources" section.
- Begin an exercise program today (see your physician first). Exercise is one of the most important ingredients to effectively manage stress and anxiety and keeps us buoyant and energized while working with heinous trauma.
- Teach your friends and peers how to support you. Don't rely upon random remarks from friends and colleagues to be helpful. Instead, let them know what is most helpful for you during times of stress and pain. You may choose to offer the same to them in a reciprocally supportive arrangement. Periodic or regular professional supervision may also be helpful, especially during a rough time.
- Develop your spirituality. This is different than going to church, although church may be part of your spirituality. Spirituality is your ability to find comfort, support, and meaning from a power greater than yourself. We have found this quality necessary for the development of self-soothing capacity. Meditation, Tai Chi, church/synagogue, Native American rituals, journaling, and workshops are all examples of possible ways in which to enhance one's spirituality.
- Bring your life into balance. Remember that your best is ALWAYS good enough. You can only do what you can do so when you leave the office (after 8 hours of work)... leave the office! Perseverating on clients and their situations is not helpful to them, you, or your family. You can most help your clients by refueling and refilling yourself while not at the office. Live your life fully!
- Develop an artistic or sporting discipline. Take lessons and practice as well as play and create. These are integrative and filling experiences. It is paradoxical that when we feel drained that we need to take action instead of sinking into the sedentary "couch potato." Taking action will be rewarded with a greater sense of refreshment and renewal, while activity avoidance will leave us even more vulnerable to the effect of stress the next day.
- Be kind to yourself. If you work with traumatized individuals, families, and/or communities, your life is hard enough already. You do not need to make it more difficult by coercive and critical self-talk. In order to become and remain an effective traumatologist your first responsibility is keeping your instrument in top working condition. Your instrument is YOU, and it needs to be cared for.
- Seek short-term treatment. A brief treatment with some of the accelerated trauma techniques (i.e., EMDR) can rapidly resolve secondary traumatic stress symptoms. If you would like assistance in finding a Certified Compassion Fatigue Specialist in your area, please contact the International Traumatology Institute at (813) 974-1191.

colleague who has committed suicide) and should be treated with great respect. Often, it seems, those who suffer most from compassion fatigue are those individuals who are highly motivated to bring about change and healing in the lives of the suffering. It is especially painful to witness the progressive debilitation of these loving caregivers, who are often our very close friends. Without a doubt, many hundreds, if not thousands, of caregivers and emergency service workers providing hour after hour of intensive and life-altering service to those affected by the events of September 11th will experience deleterious effects themselves from this heroic work. Finding the ways and means to both thoroughly study these effects and, maybe more importantly, provide rapidly effective and empirically validated treatment for these suffering heroes, will become a crucial task toward the completion of our nation's healing.

The good news is that the symptoms of compassion fatigue appear to be very responsive to being treated and rapidly ameliorated (Pearlman & Saakvitne, 1995; Gentry & Baranowsky, 1999). While substantially more research in this area will be required before we can offer definitive statements about the nature of treatment, prevention and resiliency with compassion fatigue, some principles and techniques discussed here offer a foundation for helping caregivers resolve their current symptoms and prevent future occurrences. Moreover, we have witnessed for numerous caregivers the symptoms of compassion fatigue becoming a powerful catalyst for change. With skilled intervention and determination, care providers with compassion fatigue can undergo a profound transformation leaving them more empowered and resilient than they were previously, and therefore better equipped to act as "givers of light."

NOTES

1. *Treatment Manual for Accelerated Recovery from Compassion Fatigue* (Gentry & Baranowsky, 1998) is available from Psych InK Resources, 45 Sheppard Ave., Suite 202, Toronto, Ontario, Canada, M2N 5W9.

2. These trials were completed with volunteers who were Marriage & Family Therapists, a trauma therapist from South Africa, and a volunteer who had been providing relief work in Sarajevo.

3. This participant uncovered a primary traumatic experience for which she was previously amnestic. She left the country before her primary or secondary trauma could be successfully addressed and resolved.

REFERENCES

American Psychiatric Association. (1980). *Diagnostic and statistical manual of mental disorders* (3rd ed.). Washington, DC: Author.

Bergin, A. E., & Garfield, S. L. (1994). Overview, trends, and future issues. In A. E. Garfield & S. L. Bergin (Eds.), *Handbook of psychotherapy and behavior change*. New York: J. Wiley.

Bloom, S.L. (2000). Our hearts and our hopes are turned to peace: Origins of the International Society for Traumatic Stress Studies. In A.H. Shalev & R. Yehuda (Eds.), *International handbook of human response to trauma. The Plenum series on stress and coping* (pp. 27-50). New York: Kluwer Academic/Plenum Publishers.

Burns, D. (1980). *Feeling good: The new mood therapy*. New York: Morrow.

Catherall, D. (1995). Coping with secondary traumatic stress: The importance of the therapist's professional peer group. In B. Stamm (Ed.), *Secondary traumatic stress: Self-care issues for clinicians, researchers, and educators* (pp. 80-92). Lutherville, MD: Sidran Press.

Cerney, M. S. (1995). Treating the "heroic treaters." In C. R. Figley (Ed.), *Compassion fatigue: Coping with secondary traumatic stress disorder in those who treat the traumatized* (pp. 131-148). New York: Brunner/Mazel.

Cherniss, C. (1980). *Professional burnout in human service organizations*. New York: Praeger.

Danieli, Y. (1982). Psychotherapists' participation in the conspiracy of silence about the Holocaust. *Psychoanalytic Psychology, 1(1)*, 23-46.

Deutsch, C. J. (1984). Self-reported sources of stress among psychotherapists. *Professional Psychology: Research & Practice, 15*, 833-845.

Farber, B. A. (1983). Introduction: A critical perspective on burnout. In B. A. Farber (Ed.), *Stress and burnout in the human service professions* (pp. 1-20). New York: Pergamon Press.

Figley, C. R. (1983). Catastrophe: An overview of family reactions. In C. R. Figley & H. I. McCubbin (Eds.), *Stress and the family, volume II: Coping with catastrophe*. New York: Brunnel/Mazel.

Figley, C.R. (1988). Toward a field of traumatic stress. *Journal of Traumatic Stress, 1(1)*, 3-16.

Figley, C. R. (1995). *Compassion fatigue: Coping with secondary traumatic stress disorder in those who treat the traumatized*. Bruner/Mazel: New York.

Figley, C. R., & Kleber, R. (1995). Beyond the "victim": Secondary traumatic stress. In R. J. Kleber & C. R. Figley (Eds.), *Beyond trauma: Cultural and societal dynamics. Plenum series on stress and coping* (pp. 75-98). New York, NY: Plenum Press.

Figley, C. R., & Stamm, B. H. (1996). Psychometric review of compassion fatigue self test. In B. H. Stamm (Ed.), *Measurement of stress, trauma and adaptation*. Lutherville, MD: Sidran Press.

Foa, E. B., & Meadows, E. A. (1997). Psychosocial treatments for posttraumatic stress disorder: A critical review. *Annual Review of Psychology, 48*, 449-480.

Foa, E. B., Dancu, C. V., Hembree, E. A., Jaycox, L. A., Meadows, E. A., & Street, G. P. (1999). The efficacy of exposure therapy, stress inoculation training and their combination in ameliorating PTSD for female victims of assault. *Journal of Consulting and Clinical Psychology, 67,* 194-200.

Folette, V. M., Polusny, M. M., & Milbeck, K. (1994). Mental health and law enforcement professionals: Trauma history, psychological symptoms, and impact of providing services to sexual abuse survivors. *Professional Psychology: Research and Practice, 25*(3), 275-282.

Follette, V. M., Ruzek, J. I., & Abueg, F. R. (1998). *Cognitive behavioral therapies for trauma.* New York: Guilford Press.

Frankl, V. E. (1963). *Man's search for meaning.* New York: Washington Square Press, Simon and Schuster.

French, G. D., & Harris, C. (1998). *Traumatic incident reduction (TIR).* Boca Raton, FL: CRC Press.

Freudenberger, H. (1974). Staff burn-out. *Journal of Social Issues, 30,* 159-165.

Gentry, J. E. (1999). *The Trauma Recovery Scale (TRS): An outcome measure.* Poster presentation at the meeting of the International Society for Traumatic Stress Studies, Miami, FL.

Gentry, J. E., Baranowsky, A., & Dunning, K. (1997, November). *Accelerated Recovery Program for compassion fatigue.* Paper presented at the meeting of the International Society for Traumatic Stress Studies, Montreal, QB, Canada.

Gentry, J., Baranowsky, A., & Dunning, K. (in press). The accelerated recovery program for compassion fatigue. In C. R. Figley (Ed.), *Compassion fatigue II: Treating compassion fatigue.* New York: Brunner/Mazel.

Gentry, J., & Baranowsky, A., (1998). *Treatment manual for the Accelerated Recovery Program: Set II.* Toronto: Psych Ink.

Gentry, J. E., & Baranowsky, A. (1999, November). *Accelerated Recovery Program for Compassion Fatigue.* Pre-conference workshop presented at the 15th Annual meeting of the International Society for Traumatic Stress Studies, Miami, FL.

Gentry, J. E., & Baranowsky, A. B. (1999a). *Compassion satisfaction manual: 1-Day group workshop, Set III-B.* Toronto, CN: Psych Ink.

Gentry, J. E., & Baranowsky, A. B. (1999b). *Compassion satisfaction manual: 2-Day group retreat, Set III-C.* Toronto, CN: Psych Ink.

Gentry, J. E. (2000). *Certified compassion fatigue specialist training: Training-as-treatment.* Unpublished doctoral dissertation. Florida State University, Florida.

Gentry, J. E. (2001). *Traumatology 1002: Brief treatments.* Tampa, FL: International Traumatology Institute.

Gold, S. N. & Faust, J. (2001). The future of trauma practice: Visions and aspirations. *Journal of Trauma Practice, 1*(1), 1-15.

Grosch, W. N., & Olsen, D. C. (1994). Therapist burnout: A self psychology and systems perspective. In W. N. Grosch & D. C. Olsen (Eds.), *When helping starts to hurt: A new look at burnout among psychotherapists.* New York: W.W. Norton.

Haley, S. (1974). When the patient reports atrocities. *Archives of General Psychiatry, 39,* 191-196.

Herman, J. L. (1992). *Trauma and recovery.* New York: Basic Books.

Holmes, D. & Tinnin, L. (1995). The problem of auditory hallucinations in combat PTSD. *Traumatology–e: On-line Electronic Journal of Trauma, 1*(2). Retrieved from <http://www.fsu.edu/~trauma/art1v1i2.html>.

Jung, C. G. (1907). The psychology of dementia praecox. In M. Fordham, G. Adler, & W. McGuire (Eds.), *The collected works of C.G. Jung, H. Vol. 3*. Bollingen Series XX, Princeton: Princeton University Press.

Karakashian, M. (1994). Countertransference issues in crisis work with natural disaster victims. *Psychotherapy, 31*(2), 334-341.

Lindy, J. D. (1988). *Vietnam: A casebook*. New York: Brunner/Mazel.

McCann, I. L., & Pearlman, L. A. (1990). Vicarious traumatization: A framework for understanding the psychological effects of working with victims. *Journal of Traumatic Stress, 3*(1), 131-149.

McNally, V. (1998, November 7-8). *Training of FBI employee assistance professionals and chaplains at FBI headquarters*. Washington, D.C.

Marmar, C. R., Weiss, D. S., Metzler, T. J., Delucchi, K. L., Best, S. R., & Wentworth, K. A. (1999). Longitudinal course and predictors of continuing distress following critical incident exposure in emergency services personnel. *Journal of Nervous and Mental Disease, 187*(1), 15-22.

Maslach, C. (1976). Burnout. *Human Behavior, 5*, 16-22.

Maslach, C. (1982). Understanding burnout: Definitional issues in analyzing a complex phenomenon. In W. S. Paine (Ed.), *Job stress and burnout: Research, theory and intervention perspectives* (pp. 29-40). Beverly Hills, CA: Sage Publications.

Maslach, C., & Goldberg, J. (1998). Prevention of burnout: New perspectives. *Applied and Preventive Psychology, 7*, 63-74.

Matsakis, (1994). *Vietnam wives: Facing the challenges of life with veterans suffering post-traumatic stress*. New York: Basic Books.

Mitchell, J. (1995). The critical incident stress debriefing (CISD) and the prevention of work-related traumatic stress among high risk occupational groups. In G. Everly (Ed.), *Psychotraumatology: Key papers and core concepts in post-traumatic stress*. New York: Plenum Press. 267-280.

Norman, J. (2001). The brain, the bucket, and the schwoop. In E. Gentry (Ed.), *Traumatology 1001: Field traumatology training manual*. Tampa, FL: International Traumatology Institute.

Pearlman, L. A., & Saakvitne, K.W. (1995). *Trauma and the therapist: Countertransference and vicarious traumatization in psychotherapy with incest survivors*. New York: W.W. Norton.

Pearlman, L. A. (1995). Self-care for trauma therapists: Ameliorating vicarious traumatization. In B. H. Stamm (Ed.), *Secondary traumatic stress: Self-care issues for clinicians, researchers, and educators* (pp. 51-64). Lutherville, MD: Sidran Press.

Pole, N., Best, S. R., Weiss, D. S., Metzler, T. J., Liberman, A. M., Fagan, J., & Marmar, C. R. (2001). Effects of gender and ethnicity on duty-related posttraumatic stress symptoms among urban police officers. *Journal of Nervous and Mental Disease, 189* (7), 442-448.

Salston, M. G. (2000). *Secondary traumatic stress: A study exploring empathy and the exposure to the traumatic material of survivors of community violence*. An unpublished dissertation. Florida State University, Florida.

Saakvitne, K. W. (1996). *Transforming the pain: A workbook on vicarious traumatization*. Norton: New York.

Schauben, L. J., & Frazier, P. A. (1995). Vicarious trauma: The effects on female counselors of working with sexual violence survivors. *Psychology of Women Quarterly, 19*, 49-64.

Sedgewick, D. (1995). *Countertransference from a Jungian perspective (transcript of a lecture given at Grand Rounds to the Department of Psychiatric Medicine, University of Virginia).* Retrieved from the C. G. Jung Page, World Wide Web: <http://www.cgjung.com/articles/roundsx.html>.

Sexton, L. (1999). Vicarious traumatization of counselors and effects on their workplaces. *British Journal of Guidance and Counseling, 27*(3), 393-303.

Shalev, A., Bonne, O., & Eth, S. (1996). Treatment of posttraumatic stress disorder: A review. *Psychosomatic Medicine, 58*(2), 165-182.

Salston, M. D. (1999). *Compassion fatigue: Implications for mental health professionals and trainees.* A defended critical review at Florida State University.

Schnarch, D. M. (1991). *Constructing the sexual crucible: An integration of sexual and marital therapy.* New York: Norton.

Shapiro F. (1989). Efficacy of the eye movement desensitization procedure: A new treatment for post-traumatic stress disorder. *Journal of Traumatic Stress, 2*(2), 199-223.

Shapiro, F. (1995). *Eye movement desensitization and reprocessing: Basic principles, protocols and procedures.* New York: The Guilford Press.

Stamm, B. H. (1995). *Secondary traumatic stress: Self-care issues for clinicians, researchers, and educators.* Lutherville, MD: Sidran.

Sussman, M. (1992). *A curious calling: Unconscious motivations for practicing psychotherapy.* New Jersey: Jason Aronson Inc.

Tinnin, L. (1994). *Time-limited trauma therapy: A treatment manual.* Bruceton Mills, WV: Gargoyle Press.

van der Kolk, B. (1996). The black hole of trauma. In B. A. van der Kolk & A. C. McFarlane (Eds), *Traumatic stress: The effects of overwhelming experience on mind, body, and society* (pp. 3-23). New York: The Guilford Press.

Wilson, J., & Lindy, J. (1994). *Countertransference in the treatment of PTSD.* The Guilford Press: New York.

September 11 and Its Impact on People Around the Globe

Lenore Meldrum

SUMMARY. The type of "man-made disaster" represented by the September 11, 2001 attacks was different from any other that people in most parts of the world had experienced. In the absence of empirical data from which to assess the likely long-term impact of these attacks, trauma specialists from the world community were asked two questions:

1. Have the September 11 attacks in the United States had any impact on the people you see professionally?
2. From your professional observation have the attacks had any impact on the general population?

Responses were received from the United Kingdom, Australia, Belgium, Argentina, Israel, Canada, and Turkey, and are presented in their en-

---

Lenore Meldrum, BEd-BPsych, MMedScience, is affiliated with the Department of Psychiatry, The University of Queensland.

Address correspondence to: Lenore Meldrum, BEd-BPsych, MMedScience, 64 Hall Street, Northgate, Queensland 4013 Australia (E-mail: Lenore.Meldrum@mailbox.uq.edu.au).

In order to maintain respect for the international perspective and spirit inherent in this article, we have done minimal editing of the technical aspects of the writing. The U.S. reader will note certain variations from standard U.S. writing style. Whether due to English not being a contributor's first language, or a reflection of differences in English usage in countries other than the U.S. (e.g., many English words are spelled differently in British Commonwealth nations than they are in the U.S., and there are differences in standard usage of certain forms of punctuation), these differences have for the most part been left intact.

[Haworth co-indexing entry note]: "September 11 and Its Impact on People Around the Globe." Meldrum, Lenore. Co-published simultaneously in *Journal Trauma Practice* (The Haworth Maltreatment & Trauma Press, an imprint of The Haworth Press, Inc.) Vol. 1, No. 3/4, 2002, pp. 63-81; and: *Trauma Practice in the Wake of September 11, 2001* (ed: Steven N. Gold, and Jan Faust) The Haworth Maltreatment & Trauma Press, an imprint of The Haworth Press, Inc., 2002, pp. 63-81. Single or multiple copies of this article are available for a fee from The Haworth Document Delivery Service [1-800-HAWORTH, 9:00 a.m. - 5:00 p.m. (EST). E-mail address: getinfo@haworthpressinc.com].

tirety. Respondents indicated that their clients manifested traumatic stress reactions of varying degrees in the period immediately after the attacks, but that many clients appear to have since moved forward in therapy and begun to concentrate on recovery or on local issues.

KEYWORDS. Disaster, September 11, attacks, long-term impact, trauma specialists, world, United States, United Kingdom, Australia, Belgium, Argentina, Israel, Canada, Turkey, traumatic stress reactions, therapy, recovery

One of the major impacts of the September 11 terrorist attacks on New York and Washington DC had, for many of us, was the lasting impression that the rest of the world was no longer safe and "somewhere out there." For some days after the attacks, New York and Washington were brought right into our homes–24 hours a day on all the "free to air" and many of the cable television channels. We, in Australia, were less likely to have family or friends at ground zero than the American people–but the psychological impact on our population was intense. For people who had ever visited the World Trade Centre or utilised flights into any of the American cities involved–there was the sense–"it could have been me or mine." For those who knew no other image of the World Trade Centre, the only one they will carry for many years is the sight of the airplanes crashing into the side of the building and the resultant fireball. The psychological impact of the attacks on the reporters delivering the news to Australian audiences was addressed on television, as was the expected impact on the general population. But this type of "man-made disaster" was different from any other that people in most parts of the world had experienced–there were no data from which to draw a comparison–what would be the long-term impact? In an attempt to draw on the experiences of people around the world working in the community who are trained observers of human behaviour–the mental health professionals–I asked the following questions:

1. Have the September 11 attacks in the United States had any impact on the people you see professionally (e.g., has their levels of anxiety increased or have "old traumas" been revived)?
2. From your professional observation have the attacks had any impact on the general population (e.g., are they more security conscious–have there been any attacks on Muslim populations)?

Below are the responses I have received.

THE RESPONSES

Dr. Gordon Turnbull, BSc, FRCP, FRCPsych, FRGS, FRSA. Consultant Psychiatrist, Clinical Director–Trauma Services, The Priory Ticehurst House, East Sussex, United Kingdom Consultant Psychiatrist to the Civil Aviation Authority (CAA), Honorary Senior Lecturer to the University of Kent at Canterbury, United Kingdom

Question 1

I am in no doubt whatsoever that the September 11th terrorist attacks in the USA have adversely affected the patients that I see. This applies across the spectrum. I see patients with general psychiatric conditions such as depression, panic anxiety, phobic and generalised anxiety, as well as those suffering from post-traumatic psychopathology.

There is widely-held apprehension in the UK that there will be more terrorist attacks and that some of these are likely to be aimed at the UK. Fears that this will be likely to occur have been reinforced by the strong philosophical and practical support that was given to the US in the campaign against the Taliban regime in Afghanistan. There is a strong support for the action in Afghanistan. I have found that depressed patients have felt less optimistic about the future (personal and for the world at large) and have felt more pervasively hopeless. The attacks were generally perceived to be wanton and cruelly misplaced (especially against the 'twin towers') and generated a great deal of anger. I think that I saw bewilderment in the immediate aftermath of the attacks change into incandescent anger and outrage in those who had a normal mental state at the time. This cooled into a determination that those responsible should be hunted down and eradicated–an attitude of total intolerance. In some, the anger was defended against and converted into a feeling that the West should look again at its cultural drift and foreign policies so that we should change our way of thinking about the 'Third World' countries and be less exploitful, take the insult 'on the chin,' and try to help them more to narrow the gap between them and us. This was a less popular view in the UK than to seek retribution by military means.

Anger was therefore a major component of the collective emotional reaction to the events. In those who were already depressed, the in-rage that resulted made them more depressed. As usual in psychotherapy, the arrival of fresh sources of anger/depression has made it possible to reinvigorate the more established sources and has given an opportunity to resolve them. Therefore, the initial emotional discomfort has provided a potential platform for recovery for some patients that I have seen, who are making progress in psychotherapeutic work where they were previously 'stuck.'

Increased anxiety is another major component of the emotional reaction. Again I have seen initial discomfort lead to good therapeutic work being done. Some patients have seen their troubled lives in a different perspective. The shock felt by these patients made them realise that life gives limited opportunities and that it was important to 'make the most of things.'

The revitalisation of 'old traumas' has been a very noticeable feature in the trauma clinic. The dynamic relationship between intrusive experiences and the need to process trauma on the one hand and the avoidance of the discomfort of facing up to such work will be very familiar to 'coalface' trauma therapists. We use groups at Ticehurst to generate cohesion to facilitate sharing and normalisation and safety and to reduce the natural tendency to avoid. Our first group after September 11th found it extremely difficult to get beyond the 'storming' phase and to get into the work. There may, of course, have been other factors responsible for this but I believe that we were unable to start the group for two months after the terrorist attacks served to reinforce avoidance factors and made the group a more uncomfortable environment for them to be in. Their sense of 'victimhood' was much in evidence and difficult to work with. Interestingly, by contrast, our subsequent group had fewer members and became a cohesive unit. My impression is that the gathering together of trauma victims acted like a barometer–the greater the number the higher the pressure and vice-versa. I am aware of several examples of individuals who have rekindled symptoms of their 'old traumas,' usually incompletely processed or left aside for later, or in process at the time and settling down.

My work at the Civil Aviation Authority involves seeing aircrew and air traffic controllers amongst others. I have not been aware of any perceptible changes in these populations. This might be because of their innate, very well developed psychological defences of denial.

Question 2

Generally, I think that clinicians are finding that the British population is becoming less secure over time rather than more secure. This shows in the attitude towards working–long hours, meticulous attention to detail, competitiveness etc., etc.–leading to increased stress and more referrals. I am personally constantly amazed by the management's inability to stick to even the most basic and common sense rules with regard to managing people. Perhaps this is also a 'symptom' of increased stress.

The preceding has focused on the reactions of individuals or small groups and it is a very different matter to look at a whole population. Perhaps one can discern the impact of major events more quickly in individuals and small groups. The results may only be detectable across the population after a much longer time has passed by. Even then, generalisation about an entire population is always going to be a dangerous business. The UK is supposed to be a multicultural society and there are some who have publicly debated whether or not this is the case, the more so since September 11th. There are certainly many different ethnic groups living in the UK but the real question is whether or not there is an allegiance to the nation and the Crown, or even some ongoing integrative process that allows for genuine mixing.

I have already mentioned two different reactions to the anger and the fear that was experienced by the vast majority of people in the UK–there are the 'hawks' and there are the 'doves.' There was a real sense of shock recently when it was revealed that a British youth converted to the Muslim faith while in prison had allegedly attempted to blow up an airliner mid-Atlantic by lighting explosives concealed in his shoe. He was overpowered by crew and passengers who thereby almost certainly prevented the commission of another atrocity in the name of religion. This sense of 'shock' and 'disbelief' was one thing but followed outrage and suspicion of non-Muslim British people towards Muslims when extremist views were broadcast on national radio, famously predicting that the 'flag of Islam would one day fly over No.10 Downing Street!' Several hundred young Muslims left Britain to fight for the Taliban against British and American troops and there is much debate about what will happen if they try to return. Should they be regarded as treasonous? Will they be imprisoned? Some attacks have already been made on those Muslims who stayed at home. Muslim leaders have tried hard to declare that their people are loyal.

The actions of immigrant or non-integrated people according to religious principle is regarded as one thing but it has been a completely different matter to countenance the fact that inmates in British jails are frequently converted to the Muslim faith and the young man who nearly blew up the plane was one of those.

Perhaps it would be as well to generalise about the British character? What is that 'stiff-upper-lip' all about? I suppose it's an indication that the British like to have a good degree of control over their lives, being an island people after all. But is it not the case that the degree of control seems to be diminishing all the time? Government is increasingly centralised. Less than half of the eligible population bothers to turn out to vote at General Elections because they feel they have no real 'say' or control over the outcome. Market forces increasingly favour 'globalisation.' The introduction of the 'euro' currency that is now used by everyone else over the narrow English Channel but not by the Brits–do they know something that we don't? Should we stay out of Euroland? Should we join in? Will it lead to political union? Will that mean that we lose our autonomy?

All of these things are important. None of them are going to go away. All of these things require action. *All* of them lead to loss of control and diminished self-determination at *both* the personal and the collective levels.

Then there was September 11th. Some of the population feel, " What's the point?" Some want to see ethnic integration or " Go back home if you won't swear allegiance to the nation." Some people welcome the changes that have been brought about by September 11th, but not the event that stimulated them because the debates that rage will, hopefully, lead to a 'working through' of issues that have been on the 'back-burner' for too long and that now need to be addressed and resolved.

I suppose that this is when it is good to be part of a nation like Britain because the mixture of opinions that go into the 'melting pot' do include extreme views and all the other views spread out over the whole spectrum. Perhaps that way is the best way to achieve consensus–nobody will feel left out.

In the meantime we are witnessing a collective 'Acute Stress Disorder/Reaction' that will move on into a dimension of collective 'Adjustment Disorder/Reaction' and we have to face up to the reality of disrupted emotions before it will get better.

Denise Keenan, BA, DipAppPsych, Member of Australian Psychological Society Inc., Member College of Organisational Psychologists, MSAAH (member SA Assoc of Hypnotherapists), Director of Cognition, Adelaide, South Australia

Those clients we were seeing who were already feeling vulnerable were somewhat destabilized. They focused on it and it reinforced their view of the world as being unpredictable and unsafe. Some went so far as being teary in response to it. The CEO of a large organisation we provide an Employee Assistance Program (EAP) for sent out a memo to all staff acknowledging the impact of Sept 11 and reminding them that the EAP should be used if they felt the need. It is a good example of a caring and thinking organisational response.

Commander Erik LJL de Soir, Drs Cl Psych, DCl Psych, MMil SocSc, M. Disaster Mgt (Management), Clinical Psychologist-Psychotherapist, Senior Lecturer, Royal Military Academy, Department of Behavioral Sciences Brussels, Belgium

Cindy had been in therapy for about three months when the attacks on New York and Washington occurred. Nearly two years ago, Cindy had been the first witness of the dramatic scene of a family slaughter in which her uncle had killed–strangled to death–his two girls, drowned his wife in her bath and hung himself. First diagnosed as suffering from the chronic fatigue syndrome and then oriented toward me for a Psychotrauma therapy by a university professor in rheumatology (!). Cindy was now slowly recovering from her traumatic experiences. She followed an intense trauma therapy–twice a week–accompanied by a drug treatment and some psychomotor rehabilitation sessions. The day after the attacks on the US, Cindy came to her therapy session, completely shaky and only talking about the "events in the US." She speculated about giving up her therapy because she thought that she had no further the right to have problems with the dead of "only" four family members when in the US there seemed to be thousands of casualties. She didn't stop to make the comparison about what happened in the US and in her own family and wanted to cancel further sessions. In the meanwhile, I had been on several TV Channels, discussing the community impact of the attacks, but Cindy continued–also convinced by her mother to give up therapy and take back up her life, being happy that at least she, her husband and her two kids were still alive!–to tell someone else's story (the story of the TV victims), saying also that I certainly had other priorities instead of listening to her same stories. I didn't give up on her, kept up the planned sessions and convinced her that everybody has the right to have his own feelings about the things in his own life, and that it made no sense of giving up planned sessions, neither did we canceled sessions during the TV images on wars in other parts of the world. I told her I felt a little bit hypocrite since we didn't give the same attention to the massive slaughter of at least 500.000 people in the Rwandan genocide. She agreed and we simply continued therapy together.

Other experiences were even more interesting and indicated that the attacks on the US seemed to work as a very important trigger for fire-fighters, paramedics and policemen worldwide. I remember this story of a friend of mine, calling me up late at night, crying over the phone. He is serving as a voluntary fire officer since nearly 14 years and had a fire intervention for a very serious motor vehicle accident, the evening following Sept 11. Normally, he should have been–as always in such cases, since he lives very close to the fire department–the first at the scene of the accident, but instead, he arrived several minutes after the other fire trucks. His colleagues already started the extraction procedure of the pinched victims while he felt numb and dizzy, not really knowing what happened. The actual intervention went OK but when returning "home" he had to pull over and stop his command car beside the road. He burst into a minute-long crying and yearning, shivered and got completely out of control, being afraid that something was very wrong with him. He didn't talk about the "incident" to any of his colleagues and immediately called me upon his arrival at home. He had been watching CNN the whole afternoon and said that images of old interventions–especially interventions in which people died in cruel conditions, such as the one in which a girl lit herself on fire and walked into the fire department to cry for help–were coming back to him and haunted him. He remembered the lessons I gave them down at the fire brigade, during one of the general exercises on shocking interventions with the colleagues of the "fire and rescue stress teams," and thought that "his vase was full," too full of tears, and that he would have to stop soon. It convinced me again that people from fire and ambulance services don't want to dwell on their difficult interventions, perhaps just ready to participate in one psychological debriefing, but that by acting like this, they don't seem to fully integrate their traumatic experiences. September 11 seems to have triggered a lot of old trauma experiences in a lot of caregivers "traumatized in a latent way"–i.e. without even knowing it–who know they "can't do anything else" than cope with the direct results; anxiety levels risen to formerly unknown heights, more questions were asked during interventions (should we really go in there?–are there still people in, no, than let's stay out! etc).

An analogue situation was told me by a civil air traffic controller who also called me up, saying that the attacks on the US had triggered the whole series of near "misses"–would-be aircrashes–of the last 10 years, the time he started off as an air traffic controller. His work became a lot more difficult and the level of sick leave immediately after the attacks became an increasing problem.

Although, these attacks seem to have convinced a lot of people–leaders, commanders, etc.–of the necessity of trauma counseling. My work as a trauma counselor became much easier. After 10 years of hard work, trying to convince people of the necessity of stress and trauma support, it seems that at this moment this awareness has increased a lot and that you can immediately start with training and creating support structures, without the need of first trying to convince top management or directors.

Last anecdote: The new IBM headquarters built in Brussels are very close to the NATO Headquarters, the brand new buildings promptly seemed to become a target and caused a lot of trouble to the people who had to move to these buildings. IBM Top Management asked me to conduct stress meeting and trauma counseling sessions for managers to allow them to treat their people and react to their anxiety in a correct and adequate way.

Maybe, the biggest community impact was on children, maybe being the most important and neglected target population!

Doug Burke, BSocWk (Hons), Trauma Counsellor, Fitness Integrated Therapy, Brisbane, Australia

In my contact with veterans and their families since the September 11 attacks, I have encountered a variety of reactions. These reactions have included outright anger in a small number of cases, but by far the greater number have given serious and mature consideration to the events and their ramifications, e.g., acknowledging that the solution was far more complex than just a military reaction.

For some these concerns have been about the future involvement of Australian troops and their trepidation about what it is that these troops will encounter. A few Peacekeepers, based on their own experiences, expressed anger at the likelihood that lives would be altered forever because of political expediency around these events. For others the reactions have been an increased awareness of security issues, e.g., with large events occurring in public areas, some veterans have expressed their concerns about just how vulnerable the general population is, and how little security there is to stop any serious attempt at terrorism.

Having expressed these reactions, I was surprised to notice that in the majority of cases these events did not precipitate a re-experiencing episode for the veterans concerned. This may be an effect of treatment processes for Vietnam Veterans in that they themselves have progressed to the point where they are able to exercise more discrimination in relation to threat. A further possibility is that it may be related to a distance in time from their own experience. However, even veterans from more recent conflicts have not reacted as strongly as myself and others feared. Staff from the Vietnam Veterans Counselling Service, for example, were expecting a strong reaction from clients, but thankfully the reaction, though present, was not as intense or as large in number as anticipated.

One unexpected reaction that I encountered very soon after the tragic day was that two veterans rang to postpone their appointments at this time. Both stated in their own way that these events made them realise that their problems were minimal in comparison to what others were experiencing at that time and that they would be in contact later, but were coping for the moment.

Eduardo H. Cazabat, Psychologist, Certified Traumatologist, CETraPsiS (Centro de Estudios del Trauma Psicologico y el Stress), Buenos Aires, Argentina

Question 1

Absolutely. Every single session I have given subsequent to 9/11 has begun with references to the attack. I noticed an increase in anxiety symptoms, and a relapse in people who suffered from flight phobia. I had a former airline hostess as a client, who presented with PTSD as a consequence of a robbery, and whose symptoms worsened markedly at that time. Many patients showed psychosomatic symptoms as a result of continuous exposure to the media and consequent stress.

Question 2

Yes. For many days people became riveted by watching TV, viewing the scenes over and over again, as if they could not become convinced that such a horror had actually occurred. The images seemed to have some sort of hypnotic attraction: People were horrified by them, but were unable to stop watching them. People seemed to become "drained," and I saw an increase in sleep disturbances and anxiety symptoms. There was also a sense of hopeless and uncertainty about the future. Many people in my country went to New York during the last decade, and they tended to identify with the victims, having the feeling that "it could be me." There was a kind of Compassion Fatigue or Secondary Traumatization watching the victims (especially those leaping from the towers) or reading stories (as that of the air hostess saying good bye to her husband by cell phone). From that time on, people here in Argentina have looked for the Twin Towers in old movies or TV shows with a sad and nostalgic feeling, knowing that the world will never be the same.

Mark Creamer, PhD, Professor/Director, Australian Centre for Posttraumatic Mental Health (ACPMH), Victoria, Australia

With regards to the impact of the September 11 attacks–generalisations are unwise: Everyone reacts differently and there is a danger of self-fulfilling prophesy–if we go looking for it, we will find it. However, anecdotal reports from around Australia suggested an impact on many patients with a prior history of trauma in the period immediately following September 11th. Reactions were varied, including general distress and anxiety, fear, increased arousal, and, in a relatively small proportion of cases, reactivation of their own traumatic memories. Often people reported feelings of despair and hopelessness or, especially among veterans, extreme rage and fantasies of revenge. Some therapists reported that these latter emotions were particularly difficult for them, challenging fundamental values of compassion, tolerance, empathy, and non-violence. Some people expressed the view that, given its foreign policy and previous actions in the Middle East, "America got what it deserved," while others were concerned about Australian military involvement and the potential for young people to be used as "cannon fodder." There was considerable variation in the degree to which patients exposed themselves to news footage: Some watched it obsessively while others made great efforts to avoid media reports.

Importantly, however, most reactions to September 11th seemed to have been short lived and several therapists were surprised that the impact was not greater on their patients–certainly, they were initially upset but settled quickly. It was suggested that this may be because the events were a shared experience, with existing therapeutic structures providing a forum for expression of common emotional reactions and rapid recovery.

Professor Eli Somer, Faculty of Social Welfare and Health Studies, University of Haifa, Senior Clinical Psychologist, Director, Maytal–Israel Institute for Treatment and Study of Stress Haifa, Israel

Disclaimer: I have been on sabbatical and away from my practice since November, 2001.

Question 1

The events of September 11th had only a small effect on my clients. Some patients embarrassingly admitted that they hoped the world will have a greater empathy now for the suffering from Arab and extreme Muslim suicidal terrorism Israelis have been subjected to during the past sixty years. However, my posttraumatic patients often get triggered by the many terrorist attacks and other military hostilities the Israeli population has been subjected to.

Question 2

The horrific events of September 11 have been overshadowed by a constant chain of suicidal terrorist attacks on the Israeli civilian population. It is the latter which *have had* the most intense impact on the general population.

Israelis have been highly security-conscious for decades now, and sentiments towards Arabs have not been as trusting and respectful as one would normally expect in a pluralistic democracy.

Su Baker, MEd, Licensed Counsellor/Psychotherapist, John Abbott College, Ste. Anne de Bellevue, Canada, Independent Practice, Montréal, Canada

Question 1

In the immediate aftermath, for about two months, most of my previously traumatized patients had an increase in their post-traumatic symptoms (nightmares, flashbacks, general anxiety, increased angry outbursts, depression, etc.)–yet not one connected the dots that it was related to the attacks on the WTC and the Pentagon (Montreal is about 350-400 miles from NYC). This is not to say that they didn't talk about the attacks but they didn't realize that what they were feeling was related to the attacks–most of them had an increase in symptoms beginning a few weeks after the attacks. However, by about two months, most had returned to their previous state symptomatically.

Question 2

This is hard to say–there were some attacks in Montreal on Muslims–including a female Muslim doctor who was attacked in an elevator of one of the McGill teaching hospitals where she is a medical resident. There were a few others, but this too seems to have died down. In the college where I work part of the time, students were very unsettled by the attacks and I know that for some their semester was disrupted. There were also some who lost family members or friends. But in general, I can't say that they are more security conscious or not. Again, more in the immediate aftermath there was a sense of insecurity and people were more anxious about packages left behind on the metro (subway) and so on, but I think that this has died down to some extent. Has the general population gone back to the state that they were in before? Probably not–I think that there is a slightly higher anxiety than in the past–Canada is seen as an ally of the US (sometimes seen as a part of the US, though we most definitely are not)–and we have had terrorists among us (just yesterday two of the Al-Qaida terrorists in the video of five were identified as Canadian). So some people have some fears of reprisals on Canadian territory. But in general, it seems to me that overall, there was a spike in anxiety and then it went down, but not to where it was before.

Vedat Sar, MD, Professor of Psychiatry, Istanbul University Istanbul Medical Faculty, Director, Clinical Psychotherapy Unit and Dissociative Disorders Program, Istanbul, Turkey

The impact of September 11 events on Turkish people was twofold: Turkey has a mainly Muslim population (but a secular regime) and we have been in the deepest economic crisis of the country since its establishment. We also had experienced a severe earthquake causing a high number of casualties and economic loss. Due to this generally unhappy atmosphere, the September 11 attacks caused a general sense of insecurity as it might cause further economic instability in the country due to the international negative developments. (People are aware of the globalism in economy.)

The event did not cause individual psychological effect besides this general negative impact. Turkey has already been under attack of various terrorist organizations for a few decades. Just the activities of PKK, Kurdisch Separatist Organization, caused 30 thousand casualties in three decades. So, people are accustomed to security measures. On the other hand, most of the people in Turkey do not identify themselves with fundamentalist Islamic regimes.

John A. O'Neil, MD, FRCPC, Assistant Professor, Department of Psychiatry, McGill University, Montreal, Canada

This response is from a mixed practice: The majority of my patients (~120) are general hospital outpatients, seen about 4 times yearly; a minority are seen in 1-3/week therapy, of whom most have PTSD or DID.

Virtually all my patients reacted to the attacks with increased anxiety, and this was by no means restricted to patients whose pathology was primarily posttraumatic. Schizophrenics, bipolars, personality disorders and "normal neurotics" were all affected. At the same time, the reactions were generally quite muted in comparison to what I have seen on the US media, or heard from my US colleagues. The degree of reaction depended mostly on degree of identification. White anglophones identified most closely with the US, and reacted the most strongly. They were the most likely to have some personal contact to NYC or to someone living there. Francophones reacted less strongly, especially unilingual francophones, especially if they had never visited the USA. Patients belonging to ethnic minorities that might be identified as Arab or Afghan (this includes Christians, Muslims, Sikhs and Hindus) were especially anxious about their own security. The reaction from my Muslim patients was muted by the fact that most are North African francophones (from Morocco or Algeria), cut off from the US by language, and from Afghanistan by being from the other end of the Muslim world. My most recently and severely traumatized patients (civil war refugees from Sri Lanka, Congo, etc.) were little affected, having escaped far worse disasters.

The only "American" response, characterized by outrage that his nation had been attacked, and eagerness for revenge, was from an Iroquois Canadian who had purportedly served in the Gulf War with the CIA, and been taken prisoner, and escaped, etc. But this patient has DID, and the last time he saw me he expressed doubts about having been in the Gulf at all.

Roger Dooley, BComm, DipPsych, MA, FAPS, Clinical Psychologist, Brisbane, Australia

No doubt like many psychologists involved in providing therapy I experienced the reverberations of September 11 on my clients. In the days and up to weeks afterwards, to a person, each client had to refer to September 11 in some way in sessions. Of course I too was not immune from the impact, having been watching the late news when the crash of the second plane was shown live and stayed for hours to watch in disbelief as events of world changing nature unfolded. Consequently I often found myself in sessions revealing some of the effect on me, asking about impact on the client, or referring to the many facets of September 11 in some way as analogy or metaphor for the client's current focus of concern.

It seemed that the psychological impact reported in the early phase after September 11 fell on the two poles of optimism/pessimism. One group of clients interpreted the events as a revelation that life was indeed temporary and fragile. They commented that there was a new or more pressing realisation that they should live their life now, in a way that brought maximum satisfaction and fulfilment of goals, in which case they were finding at least a personal "perceived benefit" in the horror of the experience.

At the other pole, a group of people expressed dismay and almost defeat at the news. It appeared to shatter whatever degree of positiveness and confidence they held that the world was a good place, that people were humane and kind, and that there was a better future that they could expect. A feeling of helplessness seemed paramount in the response being expressed.

It was difficult to discern what factors in people influenced the direction they moved along this spectrum. Some clients who were already making good progress took positive meanings from the experience, just as others who were at the bottom seemed to use it as an ignition point to motivate progress. In contrast, others who were doing well had their motivation set back. However, in the latter case it seemed that this was a temporary effect and momentum was able to be recovered.

One notable effect was the increase in importance of family attachment. Many clients felt great anxiety of being apart from family members, even for everyday activities. In some cases it took time for this fear to settle and for calm, independent behaviour to re-emerge.

From my perspective, one of the healthy effects of the September 11 events and subsequent world reactions has been to deepen the appreciation of clients for the ambiguity and contradictions in life. While virtually all opinion has been strong in terms of horror, there has been significant evidence of appreciation that rights and wrongs can be seen on both/many sides. This has enabled an opportunity to explore personal issues, for which clients were seeking treatment, with greater depth and recognition that solutions are rarely easy or clear-cut.

Roderick J Ørner, MSc, CClin Psych, FBPS Visiting Professor in Clinical Psychology, University of Lincoln, UK

Sharon E. Gardner, BSc(Hons), MSc (Health Psychology) Peter Stolz, BSc Dip (Clinical Psychology) Anna Avery, B.A. M.Sc (Clinical Psychology), Jenny Noero, MSc (Counselling Psychology), Lincolnshire, United Kingdom, Seeing But Not Wanting to Know

'The Shock of the New' is one of the more readable books by the Australian art historian Robert Hughes (Hughes 1991). This classic text was first published as a companion volume for a television series about modern art. As the title suggests, he details reactions of shock, disbelief and incomprehension evoked in the Western world by prominent artists during the twentieth century. For instance, this was Picasso's most creative phase. Inspired by ideas given cogent form in the Cubist manifesto, he and other artists hijacked prevailing constructions of perception and drove a large bus through complacent orthodoxy. They advocate a worldview that liberates perception from historical shackles that blind us to our potential for shifting sensory experience into new dimensions and raising our levels of awareness to unprecedented levels of felt intensity. The Cubist challenge to how our senses are used is no less radical than Einstein's theory of relativity is to Newtonian physics. That these two 'manifestos' should be presented to an unsuspecting public at about the same time is no coincidence.

Hughes pleads for a mobilization of courage to confront the perceptual and intellectual challenges mediated by modern art. Whilst the rigor of his argument is commendable, public reaction is defensive. As if to underline this deep reserve modern art rarely engenders more than bemused incomprehension or intellectualized outrage. In consequence opportunities are missed to carry experience into rarely explored sensory domains. We prefer our lives to unfold with untroubled linearity and dismiss radical challenges to orthodoxy for adding nothing tangible to our daily requirements.

Terrorizing the human spirit has effects every bit as devastating as Picasso depicts in 'Guernica.' Gone is the ardor once evoked by exhibitions of works by Rothko, Jackson Pollock or Magritte. Their creations are now examined as icons of a bygone age and interest centers on the originality of the images that are instantly recognizable from endlessly reproduced postcards, coffee-table picture books and mass media presentations. So, with time these paintings have become firmly embedded in our common consciousness as fashion accessories cleansed of their shocking radicalism. Little new has been learned and our Western civilization clings to views of the world that are dramatically blinkered.

When trying to make sense of the impact of September 11th on psychotherapeutic practice within our specialist service for adults we have found Robert Hughes' prescient analysis to be most enlightening. Informal peer discussion reveals a striking consensus. After the attacks on The World Trade Center and The Pentagon many patients, but by no means all, made explicit reference to feeling shocked and frightened by something new they perceived to have been unleashed on an unsuspecting world. To our surprise, explicit references to September 11th disappeared from the material brought to therapy after a few weeks. If given implicit expression we have not detected it. Looking back the sense is that patients were less preoccupied by the shock of the news than were their therapists. Therapy promptly refocused on material matters with a direct bearing upon patients' everyday lives.

But at least one major change has occurred. Our awareness of the political canvas on which therapy is conducted has been shunted into a new dimension. We can no longer maintain a stance of therapeutic neutrality to expressions of racism, bigotry and ignorance. The realization has dawned that to harbor or condone such views is dangerous for us all. It was always thus but September 11th disabused us of the perception that psychotherapy is far removed from the political forces that shape our experience of the world.

We also acknowledge that the prompt relegation of September 11th and its implications to the distant periphery of patients' preoccupations is a monumental psychological achievement–all the more so for having been effected without therapist intervention. Had this adjustment been a therapeutic goal none of us would have predicted an outcome within a matter of weeks. Rational assessment would have anticipated persistent shock and disbelief, not least because ongoing threats and dangers characterize the recovery environment. Limited scope exists for challenging feelings of anxiety or depression purportedly caused by 'negative automatic thoughts' about a US foreign policy that is pursued by means of political assassinations, a war in Afghanistan that destabilizes a precariously posed region of the world and abuses of human rights being justified to combat a brand of terrorism roundly condemned for violating its victims' fundamental human rights. From a global perspective the circumstances that nurture intense hatred of the West persist. Patients confirm the axiom that there are times when not being aware carries marked advantage. Psychotherapy should not be blinded by political correctness from exploring the psychological processes invoked to maintain a stance of 'not wanting to know.'

It has not passed unnoticed in our collegiate that this capacity to promptly effect disengagement from the shock of what has and is happening is manifested in a country that did exactly the opposite during an extended period of massive public outpourings of grief at Princess Diana's death. Although less recent this incident retains a capacity to evoke intense reactions that far exceed those engendered by events on 11th September. The personal link is with a victim perceived to have been at the mercy of cruelties and rejections perpetrated by a 'known other.' The tendency is towards identification with rather than disengagement from. But there is no radical agenda at all.

Impressions elicited by re-framing the political significance of therapy changes our experience of clinical activity. For instance, a chronically traumatized war veteran has for a number of years reported impulse control problems plus violent reenactments evoked by reminders of active military service. September 11th and its aftermath offers just such an evocative scenario. But during recent months an intensification of more frequently expressed rage is provoked by television news reports about the peace process in Northern Ireland. Most recently this occurred when democratically elected Sinn Fein representatives were allocated offices at Westminster to further promote political dialogue. Assimilating reactions to war, violence and conflict is, for some, achieved more readily than adjusting to a prospect of peaceful coexistence.

Far more elaborate models of analysis than those of linear cause and effect have to be evoked to make sense of the new canvases of observation that are a legacy of September 11th. Unidimensional explanations of the multitude of impressions formed during the current period of transition are rightly experienced as platitudes. A new reality is emergent for our modern times; one that calls for simultaneous assimilation of several different perspectives into coherent representations of the complexities conveyed by our senses. Such an aspiration may be commendable but its implementation will involve radical departures from orthodoxy. To this extent the future holds many shocks and surprises in store for us, but the challenges are not new. They are as first articulated in the Cubist manifesto a century ago.

CONCLUSIONS

It has been well established that people do not have to witness a traumatic event for that event to have an impact on their psychological well-being (Dixon, Rehling, & Shiwach, 1993; Terr, Bloch, Michel, Shi, Reinhardt & Metayer, 1999; Cantor, Mares & Oliver, 1993). In the responses to my questions all respondents indicated that their clients showed traumatic stress reactions of varying degrees in the period immediately after the attacks similar to those of the American population (Schuster, Stein, Jaycox, Collins, Marshall, Elliott, Zhou, Kanouse, Morrison & Berry, 2001). The interesting aspect of the reports is the similarity of the reporting of the longer-term outcomes–many clients appear to have moved forward in therapy and begun to look towards recovery or concentrated on local issues. Previous research conducted after the Aberfan disaster suggested enhanced social and community functioning (Williams & Parkes, 1975). Raphael (1986) reported that, after a disaster "*improvements in both community and individual social functioning may be substantial when people reevaluate their lives positively in terms of their commitment to others*" (p. 196).

There is still little we know about the long-term impact of such events as September 11–but there is a great need for the knowledge that is being gathered at the "coalface" to be recorded–so that we may learn how to care for our population and ourselves more effectively.

- Who will be available to record these findings?
- Should the details be recorded as academic research?
- How can we better share our knowledge?
- These are questions to ponder on–I don't know the answers–do you?

REFERENCES

Cantor, J., Mares, M. L., & Oliver, M. B. (1993). Parents' and children's emotional reactions to TV coverage of the Gulf War. In B. S. Greenberg & W. Gantz (Eds.), *Desert Storm and the mass media*. (pp. 325-340) Cresskill, NJ: Hampton Press.

Dixon, P., Rehling, G., & Shiwach, R. (1993). Peripheral victims of the Herald of Free Enterprise disaster. *British Journal of Medical Psychology, 66*, 193-202.

Raphael, B. (1986). *When disaster strikes: How individuals and communities cope with catastrophe*. New York: Basic Books Inc.

Schuster, M. A., Stein, B. D., Jaycox, L., Collins, R. L., Marshall, G. N., Elliott, M. N., Zhou, A. J., Kanouse, D. E., Morrison, J. L., & Berry, S. H. (2001). A national survey of stress reactions after the September 11, 2001 terrorist attacks. *New England Journal of Medicine,15*(20), 1507-1512.

Terr, L. C., Bloch, D. A., Michel, B. A., Shi, H., Reinhardt, J.A., & Metayer, S. A. (1999). Children's symptoms in the wake of Challenger: A field study of distant-traumatic effects and an outline of related conditions. *American Journal of Psychiatry, 156*, 1536-1544.

Williams, R. M., & Parkes, C. M. (1975). Psychosocial effects of a disaster: Birth rates in Aberfan. *British Medical Journal, 2*, 303-304.

The Psychology of the Terrorist: An Interview with Jerrold M. Post

Jerrold M. Post
Steven N. Gold

SUMMARY. The psychological factors that motivate terrorist acts–particularly ones such as the suicide bombings that characterized the September 11th attacks–can be especially difficult to fathom. Understanding the psychology of terrorism, however, can be invaluable in helping victims of terrorism work toward making sense of what they have been subjected to and why. Dr. Jerrold Post, a psychiatrist who specializes in political psychology and who has considerable experience in the study and profiling of terrorists, is interviewed. He explains what constitutes terrorism, its purpose, how profiling "at-a-distance" is conducted, the various categories in a typology of terrorism, and the psychological and socio-political forces that support terrorism in general and suicide bombings in particular.

Jerrold M. Post, MD, is affiliated with The George Washington University.

Steven N. Gold, PhD, is affiliated with Nova Southeastern University.

Address correspondence to: Steven N. Gold, PhD, Nova Southeastern University, Center for Psychological Studies, 3301 College Avenue, Fort Lauderdale, FL 33314 (E-mail: gold@nova.edu).

[Haworth co-indexing entry note]: "The Psychology of the Terrorist: An Interview with Jerrold M. Post." Post, Jerrold M., and Steven N. Gold. Co-published simultaneously in *Journal of Trauma Practice* (The Haworth Maltreatment & Trauma Press, an imprint of The Haworth Press, Inc.) Vol. 1, No. 3/4, 2002, pp. 83-100; and: *Trauma Practice in the Wake of September 11, 2001* (ed: Steven N. Gold, and Jan Faust) The Haworth Maltreatment & Trauma Press, an imprint of The Haworth Press, Inc., 2002, pp. 83-100. Single or multiple copies of this article are available for a fee from The Haworth Document Delivery Service [1-800-HAWORTH, 9:00 a.m. - 5:00 p.m. (EST). E-mail address: getinfo@haworthpressinc.com].

KEYWORDS. Terrorists, suicide bombings, September 11, psychology of terrorism, victims, political psychology, profiling, typology of terrorism, psychological, socio-political

For the most part, traumatologists specialize in working with those who have been exposed to trauma–the *victims*. They therefore often have an extensive understanding of the mindset of the trauma survivor. However, they usually are much less familiar with the knowledge base about the mentality of the *perpetrators* of the acts of interpersonal violence. The psychological factors that motivate terrorist acts–particularly ones such as the suicide bombings that characterized the September 11th attacks–can be especially difficult to fathom. Understanding the psychology of terrorism, however, can be invaluable in helping victims work to make sense of what they have been subjected to and why. Dr. Jerrold Post, a psychiatrist who has devoted his career to the field of political psychology, and who has considerable experience in the study of terrorist psychology and the profiling of terrorists, kindly agreed to be interviewed for this collection on the subject of the psychology of terrorism. As he makes clear in the discussion below, understanding the motivations for terrorism requires recognizing that these acts are driven not just by the psychology of the individuals who carry them out, but also by a particular type of socio-political context that supports them. This interview was conducted via telephone on January 27, 2002.

Jerrold Post, MD, has specialized in the intersection between psychology and political psychology since very early in his long and distinguished career. He is Professor of Psychiatry in political psychology and international affairs and Director of the Political Psychology Program at The George Washington University. After completing his BA and MD at Yale University, he did post-graduate training in psychiatry at Harvard Medical School and the National Institute of Mental Health and graduate training at the Johns Hopkins School of Advanced International Studies. He worked for the U.S. government for 21 years, founding and directing the Center for the Analysis of Personality and Political Behavior, which conducted assessments of foreign leadership and decision-making used to advise the President and other top government officials.

Steven N. Gold, PhD, co-editor of *JTP*, is a psychologist and professor at the Center for Psychological Studies of Nova Southeastern University, where he directs the Trauma Resolution & Integration Program. He earned his doctoral degree at Michigan State University in 1981, and his bachelor's degree at Washington University in St. Louis. He has published and presented extensively in the areas of abuse, trauma, and dissociation, and is editorial consultant and ad hoc reviewer for a number of professional journals, a Fellow of the International Society for the Study of Dissociation (ISSD), a Director on ISSD's Executive Council, Liaison of the American Psychological Association's Division of Psychological Hypnosis to the APA's Trauma Interest Group, and a member of the International Society for Traumatic Stress Studies and of the Advisory Board of the Leadership Council.

SG: The term terrorism is frequently used these days as if there is a common understanding of its meaning. However, since one group may consider the same person a terrorist who is considered a hero by another group, there's obviously some ambiguity in how it's commonly applied. How would you define the term terrorism?

JP: Well, terrorism really refers to a method rather than a cause and I think that's important to emphasize. So, it's violence or the threat of violence against non-combatants in order to gain a political, ideological, or religious goal through fear and coercion. The target audience is different from the target of the violence. It's a criminal act with symbolic goals. It's a particularly vicious species of psychological warfare with violence as communication. And if you think about it, that's a substance-free definition. And where the United Nations has run into difficulties time and time again is when they try to specify who are the terrorists. But one can be for any number of these causes, and I certainly am myself and I'm sure you are, without being willing to kill innocent lives in pursuit of these goals.

SG: Could you give an example of where you might think the term terrorism has been misapplied by a particular group referring to the acts of another group, just to clarify?

JP: Well, there's oftentimes confusion between terrorism and political violence in general and a moral relativism comes into play, so that a nation defending itself and striking out will be defined as "a terrorist nation"–a pejorative term, by no means value-neutral. Osama Bin Laden called the residents of the Twin Trade Center terrorists because they support a government that was intent on killing Muslims, so they became terrorists, stretching it to really absurd proportions. Another example, I suppose, would be Argentina, which really became a terrorist state by labeling as terrorists those who disagreed with it. Dissidents within the Argentinian population, and the period of the so-called "dirty wars" to which dissidence disappeared, and by labeling as terrorists those who opposed the government–didn't agree with it–they had done a bit of a psychological jujitsu.

SG: My understanding is that a lot of your work centers around profiling. Could you explain how the methodology of profiling is different from or similar to more standard kinds of clinical assessment where you would be doing face-to-face assessment as the majority of your methodology?

JP: Well, I had the honor and challenge regarding the U.S. government's program for assessing work leaders at a distance to help prepare the President, Secretary of State, Secretary of Defense for high level negotiations and summit meetings, as well as for helping to manage crisis situations, where leadership personalities are quite critical. And founded the Center for Analysis of Personality and Political Behavior, in which role I took the lead in developing the Camp David profiles of Menachem Begin and Anwar Sadat for Jimmy Carter, which he has credited as being extremely helpful in accomplishing what he did at Camp David. Now, really the technique is not that different from a basic clinical study from which the method is drawn–just as a psychiatric anamnesis will combine a psychologically-oriented biography with the goal of understanding psycho-genetically what were the origins of the conflict, which were to be ultimately spelled out in the social illness of the clinician. So, too, we look longitudinally at the influences that shaped a leader–the culture in which he was born, the developmental experiences, his heroes, his models, his hopes and dreams–and try to understand the experiences before becoming a leader that shaped this individual, not that would shape mental illness, but that would shape and give rise to this individual as a national leader. So it could be said that in many ways a leader is created by his people. And one of the questions [is], "Why was this particular leader selected by his followers at this moment in history?" At one moment in history it is a peacemaker that is sought, at others it is a man who will be a warrior. In looking at the biographical material, it is particularly important to be identifying the role of the mentor, the matter of first successes as a leader, first failures as a leader, for they often become really deeply engraved within the emerging of political persona. In the cross-section, many of the elements we would look at are quite similar to those we look at in a clinical case study, though we address elements beyond. So, we'd be looking at the nature of his interpersonal relationships, but also of his political relationships–the nature of his relationship with his leadership circle, crisis decision-making style, strategic decision-making style, the critical attitudes, the so-called operational code: how individuals view the nature of politics, and what are the instrumental manners of leading and of resolving conflict? Negotiating style is something else we would look at. So, it would go way beyond what would be looked at in typical clinical case study, but nevertheless, using a similar situation. Now as you note, what is missing is seeing that person face-to-face. One of the ways we can compensate for that would be to interview as many people as possible who indeed have met that leader face-to-face. One of the ways we compensate for not being able to get a biographic history from the individual himself is to read as many biographical portraits as we can, both the official biographies as well as the more authentic biographies. And some would say, "Why on earth would you want to use an official biography that is just idealized pap?" but in fact, you can almost view the official authorized biography as the individual as he would like to be seen–his ego ideal. And it is the contrast between that official biography and the unauthorized biography that represents the tension placed on the individual. We regularly look at how this individual responds to crises. Other things being equal, it is the crisis decision style, which oftentimes we're most interested in, that will predict how he will react to a crisis in the future. Let me give an example from Saddam Hussein, whom I profiled in 1991 and testified twice before Congress, before the House Foreign Affairs Committee as well as the Armed Services Committee of the Senate. Looking longitudinally at his career as leader, Saddam Hussein has justified his "revolutionary pragmatism"–his capacity to, when a political action was taken which was not proving profitable and politically advantageous, to stop on a dime and reverse himself in the service of the revolution. And in fact we opined that he could reverse himself again after the invasion of Kuwait if, and this is a double contingency, if he could preserve his face, and if he could preserve his power base. To lose your face in the Arab world is possibly losing not only your position but losing your life. However, the dynamics of the conflict, as they worked out, made it almost impossible for him to do so without a humiliating defeat. In fact, you may recall George Bush senior, then President, pounding on the table and saying, "There will be no face-saving." Moreover, there were rumors that the United States would not cease to struggle, not until Saddam Hussein was killed and his regime was destroyed–that then we would continue beyond the borders of Iraq. So there was good reason for him to believe that there was no way of him just retreating and ending the conflict. Now, I mentioned earlier the issue of the leadership circle. The reason this is so critical, to be able to understand in depth not just who they are but the nature of the relationship with the leaders–no leader really can rule a country [alone]. He gets his information from the circle around him. He executes his position through the circle around him. So a leader, if we were to measure him with conventional psychological tests, could be seen as being in touch with reality psychologically, but could be totally out of touch politically if he were surrounded by a group of sycophants who told him what he wanted to hear rather than what he needed to hear. And this of course, will be a matter not only of who is chosen but also reflects the dynamics between the leaders and the leadership circle. Let me give you a particularly chilling example. In 1982, the war that Saddam Hussein had initiated with Iran was going badly for Iraq. They needed to stop the conflict. He let this be known. But by now, Khomeini is totally obsessed with Saddam Hussein and said there would be no peace with Iraq until Saddam was out of power. He'd either have to step down voluntarily or be deposed. So Saddam called a cabinet meeting and said, "Gentlemen, we have a dilemma. Khomeini has said unless I step down, the conflict will continue; there will be no peace with Iraq unless Saddam is gone. What say you?" And everyone to a man of course said, "Oh noble Saddam, of course you must stay on as president. Saddam is Iraq. Iraq is Saddam." And then Saddam said, "No, no, no, no. I want to ask you for your frank, candid, and creative opinion." At this, this Oxford educated Minister of Health, Dr. Ibrahim said, "Well Saddam, you might want to think about temporarily leaving office until our goal of peace was achieved and then resuming the presidency"–really a very shrewd suggestion. As the story goes, Saddam thanked him gravely for his candor and had him arrested on the spot. The minister's wife went to Saddam that evening and said, "Your excellency, please return my husband to me. He's always been loyal to you. Please return my husband." And he promised her he would–as best as I can tell the only promise he's ever kept–and returned her husband to her the next day in a black canvas body bag, chopped into pieces. This powerfully concentrated the attention of the remaining ministers, who to a man assured Saddam that he should continue as president. Well, this combination of a sycophantic leadership circle and an ethno-centric attitude led Saddam regularly to miscalculate. On the one hand, he was a rational calculator, but he often miscalculated. And this is really very important to understand. But I do want to emphasize, there really is no prediction with a capital "P" here, because we're talking about an important variable in a galaxy of variables. So, that all political decisions are multiply determined. We can identify patterns, we can identify trends, but never really give hard predictions. So, for example, as the Gulf conflict played out, a lot of it had to do with the dynamic interactions between Saddam Hussein and the West in general, the United States in particular, and President Bush in particular. One of the things I thought, for example, was quite counterproductive was the tendency to personalize the conflict, so that each time this was George Bush taking on the personification of evil, and personally attacking, as George Bush, the President of Iraq, this became a real positive boost for Saddam Hussein in his part of the world. Now, I think he had the courage to stand up to the most powerful nation on earth and the President. But, when this was Saddam Hussein against a community of nations, he very much wanted to be a member of that community. And this was much more of a disincentive for him than the incentive of beating George Bush. So one has to always be looking at the cultural context. Now, that's kind of a mini-summary of profiling. But, on the basis of our success in profiling leaders of concern, the administration–when the epidemic of terrorism began in the 70s, we all remember the 1972 Munich Olympics, the seizure of the Israeli Olympic village by the radical Palestinian terrorists, all of the terrorists and the Olympic athletes were killed in the botched rescue attempt by the German authorities. That really was also dated as the beginning of the modern era of terrorism when the power of television to spread their message became so transparent, so obvious–so that a small group of individuals, by carrying out this act, could gain major international attention to their cause. And when this epidemic of terrorism began, my group was asked, "Can you take the same at-a-distance psychological profiling techniques you've used to profile world leaders and apply them to terrorist groups and their leaders?" So, we took on this task. And I think it's important to emphasize that one of our findings, which is perhaps initially counterintuitive, is that most terrorists are quite psychologically normal, that is normal in the sense of not suffering from a DSM-IV Axis I diagnosis. In fact, terrorist groups expel from their membership individuals who are emotionally unstable where they represent a security threat. Just as a Green Beret group would not wish to have an emotionally unstable member within it. And as I immerse myself in the literature of certain terrorist memoirs, and reading between the lines, it is increasingly clear that this is not a function of individual psychopathology, rather it is a function of group and organizational psychology. And we see this now I think very much in terms of the thronging groups in Israel who are lining up to join the terrorist organizations of Hamas and Islamic Jihad. During the research study we've been working on, which we are just bringing to closure, where we interviewed 35 incarcerated Middle Eastern terrorists in Israel–both secular terrorists of Fatah and 20 radical Islamic terrorists of Hamas, Islamic Jihad, and Hizbollah–it was quite striking when we asked the question concerning recruitment and why they joined, we had a befuddled response: "Well everyone was joining. It would be the strange thing to do not to join." So it's very much a social phenomenon, not representing individual pathology.

SG: Given that, to what extent have you found that there's a common psychological makeup or a common perspective across terrorists, and to what extent have you come to the conclusion that there's a variety or a typology of terrorist mentalities?

JP: That's an excellent question. I think it's really important to be thinking not of terrorist psychology as much as terrorist psychologies. And there really is a spectrum, and let me sketch out that spectrum for you. [See Figure 1.] So, across the top we have criminals, crazies, and crusaders, speaking somewhat more alliteratively. And, as I noted already, there are some individual psychopathologically disturbed terrorists acting in a political cause. But they're not members of terrorist groups or organizations–one would think of the early skyjackers of the aircrafts bound for Cuba. There is some fusion between criminal terrorists and political terrorists, and the Narco Trafficantes have taken social revolutionary terrorists and hired them as mercenaries, in fact. So, in the Andean nations of Colombia and Peru there has been a movement for some of the social revolutionary terrorists to move into the criminal pathways as a way of financing their continuing revolution, of which a striking example is FARC. [Fuerzas Armadas Revolucionarios de Columbia–in English, Revolutionary Armed Forces of Columbia]. But we will be concerned with political terrorism in this discussion. At the middle level, state terrorism concerns when the state turns the weapons of the state, which has a great deal of power–judiciary, internal police, legislature–against its own citizens. And as I noted earlier, Argentina during the "dirty wars" is one example. Another example would be Germany during the 1930s and when Saddam Hussein used nerve gas against his own Kurdish citizens, which would have been state CBW terrorism, biological weapons terrorism. The state supported terrorism is of great concern to this country. Every year there's a list put out by the state department: Iran, Iraq, Syria, Libya, Cuba, and North Korea have been on this a long time. Yemen and Somalia have at times been on it as well. And here, we need to think of the terrorist as really more as paramilitary soldiers of the state. But psychologically, sub-state terrorism is what I'd like to particularly address, and here, back again to the early days terrorism, in the early 70s and 80s the predominant two types of terrorism were (a), social revolutionary terrorism and (b) nationalist separatist terrorism. The social revolutionary terrorists were following the tradition of the anarchists of the late 19th and 20th century. Steeped in Marxist and Leninist ideology and practice, they hoped to achieve the perfect socialist state. An example

FIGURE 1. Typology of Terrorism

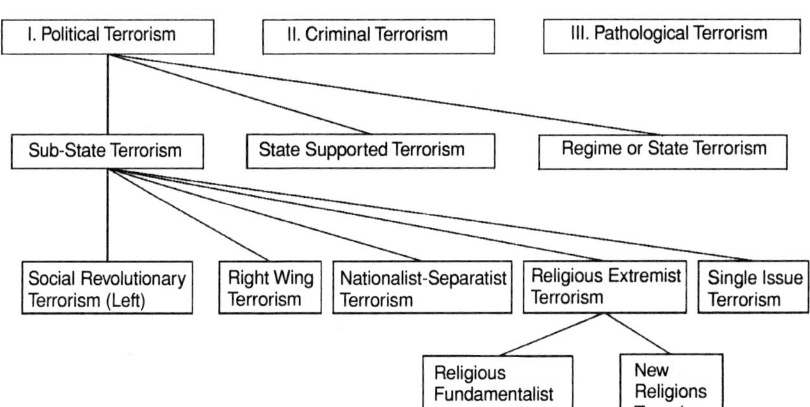

would be Nechaev's "Catechism of the Revolutionary." But, the groups that fit into this would be the Japanese Red Army, the Red Brigades in Italy, the Red Army Faction in Germany growing out of the modern Baader-Meinhoff Gang, and the United States had the Weather Underground. Again, these terrorists were in effect striking out against the generation of their families, families that were loyal to the regime. One of the German terrorists stated, "This is the generation of corrupt old men who gave us Auschwitz and Hiroshima." These groups have been on the wane since the dissolution of the Soviet Empire, but nevertheless do persist. I noted FARC earlier, the Japanese Red Army continues, the Sendero Luminosa, a Maoist group seriously weakened but it still continues. The Tupac Amaru that seized the Japanese Embassy in Peru is another example. The second major group in the 70s and 80s was the nationalist separatist terrorists. These were the terrorists who were in effect carrying on a family mission. They were a minority group within a majority society trying to carve out their own society. The radical Palestinian terrorists represent this, as do the Provos in Northern Ireland, the Provisional Irish Public Army, ETA in the Basque region of Spain, and so forth. In a generational matrix that I've developed you'll see these as mirror opposites, so that the nationalist separatist terrorists are loyal to families that are disloyal to the regime, are distant to the regime, have been damaged by the regime. They are carrying on methods that have been passed on generationally. They are seeking to free their own people from what they perceive as slavery and domination. Four or five years ago, I served as an expert witness in a trial of an Abu Nidal terrorist down here in Washington, and, very striking, this young man was 8 in 1967 when the '67 war occurred. He was living on his grandfather's farm on the West Bank and they were forced out to live in a refugee camp in Jordan. At that time, his mother said, "When I was just your age in 1948, we were living in Jaffa, in Israel, we lost our land. The same thing happened to me." In camp he was taught the only way to become a man, as a Palestinian, was to fight to regain the properties taken from your parents and grandparents. So, he was, as early as 8, 9, 10, not only being taught reading-writing-arithmetic, but was really being inducted psychologically to join the revolution and at that point, Arafat was their hero in the camp. He also started learning small weapons, how to go through a barricade, and wearing camouflage, and doing paramilitary techniques as early as his preadolescent years. When he ultimately played a lead role in the skyjacking of the EgyptAir airliner, hijacked over Malta, for him this was the crowning point of his life. He was carrying out this mission and this would help call attention to the plight of the Palestinian people. And he was intensely proud of what he had done when I interviewed him. It's an interesting example of the hatred passed on from generation to generation, hatred that is really, when it's bred in the bone, the mere signing of a Good Friday Accord or an Oslo Accord, will not easily yield to that hatred. They've been taught to hate from very early on. I was at an interesting conference at Birzeit University during the first Intafada, and there was a group of both American-trained and British-trained Palestinian child psychologists and child psychiatrists talking about the consequences of the Intafada on Palestinian children. And a Berkeley-trained clinical psychologist, a Palestinian woman, spoke about what a wonderful thing the Intafada was for the Palestinian children. At last they felt they could be proud, they could stand tall, and not just be defeated and humiliated by the enemy. Of course it was true that there was a higher incidence of bedwetting and there was no respect for parents and teachers, but what a wonderful thing it was for those children. And she was talking about children ten, eleven years old. And I was foolish enough or brave enough to say, "But my gosh, we're talking about the personality in development. Aren't we guaranteeing the generational transmission of hatred? Aren't we rewarding violence as a way of solving conflict and permanently instilling the concept of the enemy?" And at this point, the psychologist switched off and the Palestinian switched on and she answered my question and said, "Not to worry. When our people have the justice they deserve, all violence will disappear." Well, this is of course foolishness. When you've been taught to hate very early on, it will not easily yield. One of the reasons these struggles are so difficult to terminate–we keep seeing the great frustration both in the Middle East and in Northern Ireland –it just gets to the emergence of hopefulness when another act occurs. A group splits off from the mainstream, as the real IRA split off from the IRA and went back into that violence leading to a spiral of violence. But in the beginning of terrorism in the 1970s, we had these two quite different types, social revolutionary terrorists, who were striking out against generations of their parents who were loyal to the regime, and the nationalist separatist terrorists who were striking out against the regime, which had damaged their family, who were loyal to the family cause. And they were each trying to gain the attention of the West. They called attention to their cause through their acts of violence. This put a certain brake or inhibition on the extent of their violence because too much violence would be counterproductive for the cause. And they were always trying, by the way, to claim responsibility for their act, because that was quite critical to them. Then in the 1990s we saw a shift, and now some 40% of terrorist acts have no claim of responsibility made. We believe this was because these were the acts of an increasingly emphatic trend within terrorism, the radical religious fundamentalist terrorists who were particularly dangerous because (a) they weren't trying to influence the West, they were trying to expel the West, and (b) they were "true believers," who uncritically accepted the guidance of their often charismatic leader that what they were doing was in the service of God. For the radical Islamics in particular, it was in the service of Allah. But the reason they didn't claim responsibility is their audience was not here on Earth. They didn't need *New York Times* headlines or CNN stories because their audience was up above and God already knew what they had done. This is a particularly dangerous group and I see these individuals as really representing "true believers," in the sense in which Eric Hoffer wrote about in this back in the '50s, who had subordinated their own individuality to a charismatic group. And what the charismatic leader of the group said was required, indeed was religiously sanctified, they would uncritically accept. And that represents both those who followed Khomeini's leadership and human wave attacks that he helped direct in the Iran-Iraq war, those who would give their lives to truck bombings in Lebanon for Hizbollah, under the spiritual guidance of Sheikh Fadlallah and most recently, Al Qaeda under the direction of Osama Bin Laden. So it's a very dangerous movement indeed, and I think it's important to emphasize the real danger is not just Al Qaeda. The real danger is the growing attraction of radical Islam to the frustrated groups in Arab and Islamic countries who see themselves as not being able to rise within their societies. They're ready to strike out violently and have been given a religious rationale that what they are doing is in service of Allah and will make their otherwise insignificant lives quite significant as well, giving prestige and monetary reward to their families.

SG: One of the implications of what you're saying about the various types of terrorism is that there exist a variety of objectives for terrorism.

JP: Well, there exist a wide variety of objectives for terrorism. As I said, many of these would be causes to which many of us might well subscribe. There are animal rights terrorists, there are ecological terrorists, but one of my aphorisms, "the cause is not the cause," the cause is the political justification for frustrated, alienated individuals where you can strike out against the system. And I think it's very important to distinguish the legitimacy of these causes from the illegitimacy of the methods.

SG: So, that seems to suggest that one thing that may unite terrorists of various types psychologically is some form of alienation, even though that may get expressed in different ways based on the social context and the political context that they come from.

JP: I think that is accurate but insufficient in a sense, in that in terms of looking at the so-called root causes of terrorism, the issue of relative deprivation and being blocked within a society so that one cannot achieve mobility in any way. But nevertheless there are societies where there's blockage, where there's no terrorism and societies which are rather more open where there is terrorism, so it's a little bit more complex than that. But in terms of charting out how to deal with terrorism, I do think one needs to keep this very actively in mind. Security alone cannot eliminate terrorism and my kind of four-pronged solution or approach to diminishing the frequency of terrorism–when I say diminishing the frequency, you can't really eliminate terrorism without eliminating democracy. Now, that turns the state into a terrorist state. And one of the reasons the United States has been relatively free of domestic terrorism, with the exception of the bombing of the Murrah Federal Building, is that there's been so many opportunities for dissent and there's so much mobility potential within the society. So, the first prong of this four-pronged approach to dealing with this in terms of counter-terrorism would be, first, inhibit potential terrorists from joining the group in the first place. The group and organizational dynamics are very powerful. Once a person is in that pressure cooker of the group, he is increasingly shaped psychologically and sees himself in an us-versus-them struggle against the outside world. But, that can't be done just in terms of narrowly focusing on the terrorist groups. They are, as you pointed out earlier, often leading alienated and frustrated lives in their society. And what that really means is helping to find pathways for activism within that society, so that only striking out violently in this spirit of "we've got no opportunity" is not the only option when there is light at the end of the tunnel. And actually during the first Intafada, there was a sharp diminution in terrorism as the youth in these societies saw that by getting engaged in the struggle perhaps they could bring about a better future for themselves. So, number one, diminish the attraction of the paths of terrorism and create alternate paths. Secondly, produce dissension within the group. These groups are real hot houses of tension, and I think we can do a lot more to magnify the tension within the group. Thirdly, facilitate exit from the group. One of the problems is once you're in the group and you're on a most-wanted list, there's no way out. But the Italians, the British, the Basques, have created programs–the Italians have created a program called the Pentiti program, meaning "penitent"–so that the individual who wanted to leave and cooperate with the authorities would be given either a reduced jail sentence, or amnesty, not unlike our protective witness program in the United States–and in some cases would be settled in another country with a substantial financial allowance. It's very important, but most important is reducing the support for the group. At one point, the Italians, about 65% of them, thought the goal but not the means of the Red Brigade was laudable. Through a public education program, the Pentiti program, and psychological warfare, they reduced the popularity of the group from 65% to 14%, [and] put a death knell to the Red Brigade as a viable terrorist organization. So, right now, Osama Bin Laden is a hero figure for many in the alienated radical Arab world. How can we marginalize the attractiveness of Al Qaeda as an organization and de-legitimate the leadership of Osama Bin Laden, who in fact, as many have pointed out, has hijacked Islam. Islam is an inherently violent religion despite the verses he quotes that he yanks out of context, as did his intellectual mentor Khoemeni. There is no justification in Islam for the taking of innocent victims, although Bin Laden has said, "Well, if they take our innocent victims, we are entitled by Islamic law and logic to take their innocent victims." There is no justification for suicide, yet the bombers of Hamas and Islamic Jihad, those who went to their deaths gladly on September 11th, were in effect committing suicide, but they have again rationalized this away: "This is not suicide; this is istishad, martyrdom, and self-sacrifice in service of Allah." But, where is moderate Islam in terms of decrying what the radical Islam clerics and other political leaders have, like Osama Bin Laden, have been doing to their faith, because this change must come within Islam. Because right now we have in the madrassahs, the religious schools within the Arab world, are quite prolific within Pakistan in particular, a virulent brand of Islam being taught in which 8, 9, 10 year old boys are shouting, "Jihad! Jihad! Kill the Americans!"

They're being taught that America is the enemy of Islam. And this is the banner that Osama Bin Laden is trying to take, which he's been quite successful at as commander-in-chief of the Islamic world against the commander-in-chief of the corrupt modernized secular world, George W. Bush, with his able deputy prime minister Tony Blair. And Bush with Blair to their credit, have been saying, "This is not a war against Islam, it's a war against terrorism." Having said that, Bin Laden's message has had a great deal of resonance, and he's been seen in many ways–especially after the early triumph of September 11th–as really a hero to his people. And he has continued to sort of try to depict himself as the leader of the Islamic world. And it's very important we don't make this Islam versus the West. That would be a totally tragic misstep.

SG: That brings us more specifically to the suicide bombers in the September 11th attacks.

JP: In terms of suicide bombing, one of the questions we addressed in our study of the 20 radical Islamic terrorists that we systematically interviewed in Israel, in both Palestinian and Israeli jails, was how they could justify their acts of suicidal terrorism, the bombing campaigns in particular. I already mentioned the protest of one of these individuals, who said, "This was not suicide. This was istishad. Suicide was weak, was selfish, was mental illness." Istishad in Arabic means martyrdom in the service of martyrdom or self-sacrifice in the service of Allah. We had the opportunity of debriefing Hassan Salame, who was responsible for the wave of suicide bombings in Israel in 1996, in which 46 were killed. He's now serving 46 consecutive life sentences. Many would consider him responsible for the defeat of the Peres government and helping to bring Netanyahu into power. "A suicide bombing," he [Salame] said, "is the highest level of Jihad, and highlights the depths of our faith. The bombers are holy fighters who carry out one of the more important articles of faith." Another commander said, "It is suicide attacks which earn the most respect and elevate the bomber to the highest possible level of martyrdom." We also asked them about whether there was a red line, because as I noted earlier, for the secular terrorists and the social revolutionary terrorists, they had an audience. And too much violence can be counter-productive, as it was when the Real IRA after the Good Friday Accords split off from the IRA and had these terrorists attack on Omagh, when 29 women and children were killed. There was such an outcry from their constituents, they promised to never carry out violence again. So, we asked about this red line and here was a quote, "The more an attack hurts the enemy, the more important it is. That is the measure. The mass killings, especially the suicide bombings, are the biggest threat to the public and so most effort was devoted to these. The extent of the damage, the number of casualities, are of primary importance. In Jihad there are no red lines." Well, that's a similar justification promulgated within Al Qaeda, but there's one striking difference. The bombers within Israel–we didn't have the opportunity of interviewing them–they were quite inaccessible to interviewing having been killed. We talked to these commanders and the bombers in Israel, [were] 17 to 22 in age, uneducated, unemployed, unmarried–unformed youth really. Once they came into the hands of the group they were never let out of the group and were psychologically shaped, one might say brainwashed, to believe that they could make something significant out of their otherwise bleak lives. They would be enrolled in the hall of martyrs, their parents would gain prestige and monetary rewards, by carrying out an act of suicide terrorism. As I mentioned, they were never let out of the group's sight, even on the night before an action. They would be–someone [would be] sleeping in the same room to make sure they didn't backslide, and would be actually physically escorted to the site of the suicide bombing, be it shopping mall or pizza parlor or bus or whatever. In vivid contrast to those in United States, who were older, highly educated and in several cases–[Mohammed] Atta for example, had two master's degrees from a technological university in Hamburg –they came from a rather comfortable middle-class background either in Saudi Arabia or in Egypt. But most importantly, they had been on their own in the West for upwards of 7 years. That's a striking contrast to these youth who were not let alone for a moment. So they were exposed to all of the opportunities of the West, didn't just have a stereotype there. And were blending in quite successfully, but all the time keeping within them, like a laser beam focused on their mission, that this was all in the service of carrying out their mission for Allah and that they would be giving their lives while taking thousands of casualties. Well this is without question a remarkable difference. In the Al Qaeda handbook, which I obtained when I served as an expert witness in the trial last spring of the Al Qaeda terrorist bombing of our embassy in Tanzania and Kenya, was a partial explanation of how they could do it. They were called you may recall hypocrites. They were clean-shaven, they weren't praying, they weren't fasting, they did not seem to be living up to the requirements of good Muslim men. "Lesson 8, Member Safety, Measures that Should be Taken by the Undercover Members: (1) not reveal his true name; (2) have a general appearance that does not indicate Islamic orientation–beard, toothpick, book, long shirt, small Koran; (3) be careful not to mention the brothers' common expression or show their behavior, their special praying appearance ('May Allah reward you,' 'Peace be on you') while arriving or departing; (4) avoid visiting Islamic places–mosques, libraries, Islamic fairs." It goes on to say not to fast in such a way as to call public attention to yourself, to reduce the frequency of praying. Then in lesson 11, it asks an important question, "How can a Muslim spy live among enemies if he maintains his Islamic characteristics? How can he perform his duties to Allah and not want to appear Muslim? Concerning the issue of clothing and appearance, the appearance of true religion, Ibn Taimia, may Allah have mercy on him, and said, 'If a Muslim is in a combat or Godless area, he is not obligated to have a different appearance from those around him.' The Muslim man may prefer or even be obligated to look like them, provided his actions bring a religious benefit. Resembling the polytheist in religious appearance is a kind of necessity, permits the forbidden, even though their forbidden acts are basically prohibited." It basically goes on to say that Allah will forgive you for not leading a good Muslim life as prescribed in the Koran because what you're doing is in the service of Allah. It's in the service of Jihad. This book is really quite remarkable because it justifies in quite extraordinary ways, always using verses from the Koran, acts which are really pretty dreadful. There's one section, "Guidelines for Beating and Killing Hostages." They cite personality characteristics for members of special tactical operations, "tranquility and a calm personality–that allows coping with psychological trauma such as those of the operations of blood shed or mass murder. Likewise, the ability to withstand reverse psychological trauma, such as killing one or all members of his group. He should be able to proceed with the work with equanimity." It's almost a recipe, isn't it, for a psychopathic personality? The dedication of the Al Qaeda I find quite remarkable too. Again, all of these people are reading, "in the name of Allah, the merciful and the compassionate, those champions who avowed the truth day and night and wrote with their blood and suffering these phrases. The confrontation that we are calling for with the apostate regime does not know Socratic debates, Platonic ideals, nor Aristotelian diplomacy. But it knows the dialogue of bullets, the ideals of assassination bombing and destruction and the diplomacy of the cannon and the machine gun. Islamic governments have never and will never be established for peaceful solutions and cooperative counsel. They're established, as they always have been, by pen and gun, by word and bullet, by tongue and teeth."

And indeed, part of the explanation for the terrorists in the United States is they were totally captivated by the rhetoric of Osama Bin Laden, who specializes in the pen, the word, and the tongue. This is from his fatwa of 1998, "The Jihad Against the Jews and Crusaders": "In compliance with God's order we issue the following fatwa to all Muslims: The ruling to kill the Americans and their allies, civilian and military, is an individual duty for every Muslim who can do it in any country in which it is possible to do it, in order to liberate the al-Aqsa Mosque, the holy Mosque of Mecca, from their grip, in order for their armies to move out of all of the lands of Islam, defeated and unable to threaten any Muslim. This is in accordance with the words of almighty God, and fight the pagans altogether as they fight you altogether and fight them until there is no more tumult or oppression." And this I find quite striking. "We, with God's help, will call on every Muslim who believes in God and wishes to be rewarded to comply with God's order to kill the Americans." It's not Osama Bin Laden's orders to kill the Americans, but "God's order to kill the Americans and plunder their money wherever and whenever they find it." Now the question's been asked, "What will happen when Osama Bin Laden goes?" And the chilling answer is, I believe, that Al Qaeda will assuredly continue and even more so radical Islam will continue, which is really the greatest threat. Because unlike other charismatic terrorist leaders–the two most prominent examples are Guzman, the leader of the Shining Path in Peru, and Sendero Luminosa and Ocalan, leader of the PKK in Turkey–when both of these charismatic leaders were caught by the authorities, it was a mortal blow to their organizations. In contrast, Osama Bin Laden, perhaps as a consequence of his business school training in Jita, in the university, where he came under the influence of the hero of the radical Arab world Abdullah Azzam. He should really be seen as the chairman of the board of this holding company of semi-autonomous terrorist organizations, a corporation which he has grown through mergers and acquisitions. He has appointed a successor, which other charismatic leaders haven't– Zawahiri, a physician who is his number-two man–and he has a real leadership structure. So if he does die–and it is reported that he is seriously ill–fairly seamlessly the reins of power will pass on to Zawahiri. However, Zawahiri too was reported killed three weeks ago, although [this was] not confirmed. If the top leadership circle was all caught or killed, then you still wouldn't have the end of Al Qaeda because you have some 69 cells now throughout the world and you would be devolving towards semi-independent functioning, but these groups would still continue. So, we have a long, hard struggle ahead.

SG: Let me ask you this one last question: Is there anything that you haven't mentioned so far that you feel would be particularly useful for traumatologists who primarily work, not with perpetrators of violence such as terrorism, but with victims of violence, including terrorism, to know and understand?

JP: To the degree that understanding helps make sense for individuals bewildered for how violence can be delivered to innocent victims, I think this is extremely important, but it also emphasizes the collective experience. I've been working with a number of individuals who have been working collectively with the victims of political violence in Cambodia, in Kosovo, in Bosnia. And not feeling stigmatized as individuals but to belong to a group that has been attacked by another, some national group that is seeking to find, to justify its own ends, gives a degree of solidarity, which is quite important. And working with family structures can also be important too. It's really important that we interrupt the cycle of violence, because violence begets violence begets violence. And one cannot confuse traditional techniques of treating people, individuals individually, but must look at helping them achieve a group identity.

REFERENCES

Post, J. M. (1990). Terrorist psycho-logic: Terrorist behavior as a product of psychological forces. In Reich, W. (Ed.), *Origins of terrorism: Psychologies, ideologies, theologies, states of mind* (pp. 25-40). New York: Cambridge University Press.

Post, J. M. (2000). Terrorist on trial: The context of political crime. *Journal of the American Academy of Psychiatry & the Law, 28 (2),* 171-178.

Post, J. M. (2000, November 15). *The mind of the terrorist: Individual and group psychology of terrorist behavior.* Testimony prepared for Sub-Committee on Emerging Threats and Capabilities, Senate Armed Services Committee.

The Impact of Terrorism on Children: Considerations for a New Era

Robin H. Gurwitch
Betty Pfefferbaum
Michael J. T. Leftwich

SUMMARY. Terrorism is an extreme form of violent trauma made worse by being of human design. Following the terrorist attacks of September 11, 2001, the United States and the entire world entered into a new era in history. As much as adults seek to protect children from harm, their lives are too often touched by trauma, including terrorism. It is essential to examine and synthesize the findings of previous research regarding terrorism and trauma in order to guide our mental health work with children and families, particularly in the aftermath of recent terrorist events. Post Traumatic Stress Disorder symptoms in children affected by terrorism are high, with other common long-term consequences such as depression, anxiety, behavior, and developmental problems. Terrorism also raises unique trauma consequences for children. How children responded after the bombing of the Murrah Federal Building in Oklahoma City is reviewed in this paper. Although children of all ages had and have reactions to the terrorist trau-

---

Robin H. Gurwitch, PhD, is affiliated with the University of Oklahoma Health Sciences Center.

Betty Pfefferbaum, MD, JD, is affiliated with the University of Oklahoma Health Sciences Center.

Michael JT Leftwich, PhD, is affiliated with Emporia State University.

Address correspondence to: Robin H. Gurwitch, PhD, University of Oklahoma Sciences Center, Department of Pediatrics, 1100 NE 13th Street, Oklahoma City, OK 73117 (E-mail: robin-gurwitch@ouhsc.edu).

[Haworth co-indexing entry note]: "The Impact of Terrorism on Children: Considerations for a New Era." Gurwitch, Robin H., Betty Pfefferbaum, and Michael J. T. Leftwich. Co-published simultaneously in *Journal of Trauma Practice*. (The Haworth Maltreatment & Trauma Press, an imprint of The Haworth Press, Inc.) Vol. 1, No. 3/4, 2002, pp. 101-124; and: *Trauma Practice in the Wake of September 11, 2001* (ed: Steven N. Gold, and Jan Faust) The Haworth Maltreatment & Trauma Press, an imprint of The Haworth Press, Inc., 2001, pp. 101-124. Single or multiple copies of this article are available for a fee from The Haworth Document Delivery Service [1-800-HAWORTH, 9:00 a.m. - 5:00 p.m. (EST). E-mail address: getinfo@haworthpressinc.com].

mas, these may be mediated by different variables. Furthermore, the new threat of invisible agent attacks may further complicate trauma reactions in children. Research and interventions with children must be conducted on all levels (individual, family, school, community, and public policy) to effectively meet the needs of our next generation. *[Article copies available for a fee from The Haworth Document Delivery Service: 1-800-HAWORTH. E-mail address: <getinfo@haworthpressinc.com> Website: <http://www.HaworthPress.com>*

KEYWORDS. Terrorism, violent trauma, attacks, September 11, United States, children, research, mental health, families, harm, Post Traumatic Stress Disorder, PTSD, depression, anxiety, behavior problems, developmental problems, Murrah Federal Building, Oklahoma City, threat, trauma reactions, interventions, school, community, public policy

Terrorism is an extreme form of violent trauma made worse by being of human design. A primary aim in its attack of innocents is to demoralize and undermine the sense of security of a group, a community, or a country (Gurwitch, Sitterle, Young, & Pfefferbaum, in press). Until recently few major terrorist incidents had occurred in the United States. The deadliest act of terrorism had been a domestic incident in Oklahoma City in 1995, where the Murrah Federal Building had been bombed and 168 people were killed with hundreds more injured (Sitterle & Gurwitch, 1999). On September 11, 2001, that changed. In coordinated, unprecedented attacks, highjacked airliners crashed into the World Trade Center, and the Pentagon, and another attempt, was thwarted as a plane crashed into a field in Pennsylvania. The aftermath was horrific with over 3,000 dead or missing and many thousands more injured. A stunned nation and world watched as events unfolded. Even as the country was in a state of shock and utter disbelief, the President responded with a call for a war on terrorism. Nations from around the world pledged support. Thus, a new era in history had begun.

As the United States and the world entered this new phase of history, questions regarding the potential impact of the attacks were raised. One area of concern was mental health needs, particularly as related to children. The empirical literature on the psychological impact of terrorism is sparse; the literature related to children is even more so. The existing literature is drawn primarily from war-torn countries where acts of terrorism are more common (e.g., Almqvist & Brandell-Forsberg, 1997;

Ayalon, 1983a; Ayalon, 1983b; Fields, 1982). The present article reviews what is known about the impact of terrorism on children and the mental health concerns they may face in the immediate future. First, child trauma research emanating from the Okalahoma Murrah Federal Building terrorist attack is presented. Second, these findings are integrated with the research on risk and mediating factors of child trauma symptoms. Finally, the relevance of prior child trauma research to the current aftermath of the September 11th bombings is discussed.

TERRORISM AND POSTTRAUMATIC STRESS SYMPTOMS IN CHILDREN

The Diagnostic and Statistical Manual of Mental Disorders-IV (DSM-IV) (American Psychiatric Association, 1994), places the lifetime prevalence of Post-Traumatic Stress Disorder (PTSD), based on community studies, at between 1% and 15%. However, in a review of the terrorism literature pertaining to children, Gurwitch and colleagues found a range of 28% to 50% (Gurwitch et al., in press). The terrorist actions of September 11, 2001, can be considered acts of political terrorism. Researchers have suggested that victims of such terrorism show high rates of unremitting PTSD, even with treatment, as well as other long term consequences related to the events (Almqvist & Brandell-Forsberg, 1997; Desivilya, Gal, & Ayalon, 1996; Nadar, Pynoos, Faibanks, & Frederick, 1990; Swenson & Klingman, 1993). Consequences of this type of trauma include depression, anxiety, behavior and developmental problems (Elbedour, Baker, Shalhoub-Kevorkian, Irwin, & Belmaker, 1999; Trappler & Friedman, 1996). Many of these effects are similar to those associated with natural disasters or violence (Gurwitch, Sullivan, & Long, 1998; Osofsky, 1997; Perry, 1997; Vogel & Vernberg, 1993). Terrorism raises other unique consequences as well including concerns about security, trust, and outlook for the future (Gurwitch et al., in press; Macksond, Dyregrov, & Raundalen, 1993).

OKLAHOMA CITY

Children do not uniformly respond to stressful life events. Developmental differences may play a paramount role in determining responses to trauma. The following sections present data that identify posttraumatic stress (PTS) responses of children exposed to the Oklahoma City bombing of the Murrah Federal Building by age group.

School-Aged Children

Following the bombing in Oklahoma City, an effort was made to assess children's post-traumatic stress (PTS) symptoms. Approximately 3200 middle and high school students were screened seven weeks after the attack and nearly 1200 elementary school students (third through fifth grades) were assessed at 8-10 months after the event (cf. Gurwitch, 2001; Gurwitch, Leftwitch, Cote, Messenbaugh, & Pfefferbaum, 1999; Gurwitch, Leftwich, & Messenbaugh, 2001; Gurwitch, Leftwich, Pfefferbaum, & Pynoos, 2000; Gurwitch, Sitterle, Young, & Pfefferbaum et al., in press; Pfefferbaum, Gurwitch, McDonald, Leftwich, Sconzo, Messenbaugh, & Shultz, 2000; Pfefferbaum, Nixon, Tucker, Tivis, Moore, Gurwitch, Pynoos, & Geis, 1999; Pfefferbaum, Nixon, Krug, Tivis, Moore, Brown, Pynoos, Foy, & Gurwitch, 1999). The survey instrument included items related to demographics, an exposure questionnaire, and PTSD symptoms that were assessed using the Impact of Events Scale-Revised (Horowitz, 1979; Weiss & Marmar, 1997). The results are summarized below.

Children who had suffered personal loss of a family member had greater PTS symptoms than those who lost no one in the bombing. In both the middle and high school and the elementary samples, girls endorsed more PTS symptoms than did boys. For the older children, the retrospective report of initial arousal and emotions related to the bombing was significantly correlated with later PTS symptoms. Approximately 34% of the middle and high school sample remained worried about the safety of self and family two months after the attack, with 15% of the children not feeling safe at all. Approximately 75% of those experiencing a loss within the family remained worried. At approximately one year post-bombing, the elementary school children also remained worried, with 33% of the sample endorsing safety and worry items. Nearly 20% of the youngsters reported difficulty in reducing anxiety when confronted with reminders of the bombing as well as problems with concentration.

The Oklahoma City bombing was of human design. Oklahoma children across the age range expressed discomfort in their feelings about the perpetrator of the trauma. Given that the September 11th terrorist attacks were orchestrated and carried out by persons of Middle Eastern descent and the location of the war now being waged, it is important to consider how children across the country may be feeling about the perpetrators and people of similar ethnicity.

As television coverage of the bombing was extensive, children were asked about viewing habits in the immediate aftermath of the event. The amount of television viewing was significantly correlate with PTS symptoms in both the older and younger children; this finding was independent of familial loss. This finding was also a significant correlate in middle school children who lived 100 miles from Oklahoma City assessed two years after the bombing. They continued to report PTS symptoms with almost 20% of the children reporting that problems related to the bombing impaired their functioning.

Infant and Preschool Children

In addition to the screenings completed in the Oklahoma City School, qualitative data were obtained from a special population relatively neglected in the literature–infant through preschool year-aged children. As children in this age group can not complete paper and pencil measures or respond to interview questions, they are often absent from research samples and are rarely described in qualitative reports about traumas (Scheeringa et al., 1995). When the terrorist bombing of the federal building in Oklahoma City destroyed the daycare center located in the building it also caused extensive damage to the YMCA building adjacent to ground zero. This building also housed a daycare facility. Fortunately, none of the 52 children at the YMCA building were killed, but the majority sustained cuts and bruises, some children requiring stitches. Once outside of the destroyed building, the children watched the immediate aftermath of the event: fires, screaming, crying, and fleeing injured people, thick smoke, and the work of rescue personnel. Sirens were a constant sound. Children also saw their teachers and peers bloodied by injuries and crying or distressed.

Within a few weeks of the attack, the daycare center was moved to a bucolic setting within the Oklahoma City limits. At the request of YMCA personnel and the Oklahoma Office of Child Care, a team of mental health professionals headed by a psychologist (RHG) from the University of Oklahoma Health Sciences Center began educational and supportive services with the staff, families, and children in the daycare center. This team spent over three months in daily contact with the center and gradually less time over the next nine months. Observations and information obtained from staff and parents provided insight into how the youngest victims of a terrorist action may fare. Furthermore, consultations and brief interventions at child care centers around the Oklahoma City area also provided useful information. As information related to this age group is scarce in the literature, the descriptive findings are provided in detail below.

Infants

At the time of the bombing, eight infants under twelve months of age were present in the YMCA facility. These youngest victims of the bombing displayed a range of reactions. Perhaps the most significant was in the area of sleep. Parents and staff reported that the infants had greater difficulty falling and staying asleep. When asleep, the infants were often observed to twitch, move, and grimace. They reportedly awoke more irritable than had been observed prior to the bombing. Nightmares related to their infants were common. The majority of the infants were sleeping in their parents' bed. Parents reported that they felt better having their infants within reach. These behaviors continued for several months after the bombing.

Both parents and child care staff reported infants as being more irritable and fussy. Loud noises seemed more disturbing to the infants than they previously had. Staff noted that prior to the bombing, the infants could generally sleep through disturbances or when awake, ignore them. After the incident, the staff noted increased startle responses in the infants. Calming and soothing measures were needed at a high frequency. Parents also noted an increase in the need to calm their infants.

In addition to changes in the infants, the adults also reported changes in their own behaviors. Staff and parents acknowledged increased feelings of stress, thoughts of the bombing, anxiety, and worry. Parents also acknowledged worry associated with separation. Sleep disturbances were common among the parents. It is likely that the reactions of these very young victims were exacerbated by parental or caregiver reactions. Indeed, experts in trauma and the preverbal child emphasize the importance of the interaction between the caregiver and the infant (Gaensbauer, 1995).

One to Two Year Old Children

There were approximately twelve toddlers (1-2 years of age) in the relocated YMCA during the observation period. Again, staff and parents reported problems with children's sleep as well as an increase in clinging behaviors. Loud noises appeared particularly troublesome for these youngsters. Unfortunately, their relocated room was initially a floor below the YMCA weight room. With any loud noise, the majority of the children appeared to freeze and then to cry, searching for a familiar caregiver. Irritability was also noted in these children. Aggressive play was observed by team members above what would be expected for children of this age. Regressive behaviors also occurred; for example, a return to the bottle was noted in many of the toddlers. Parents admitted that they were more likely to "baby" these toddlers after the bombing than they had prior to the terrorist actions. Separation was hard for many of the parents. Like the infants, sleep in the parental bed was not uncommon. Like parents of infants, parents of toddlers interviewed by team members endorsed post-traumatic stress symptoms including re-experiencing the event, sleep disturbances, mood changes, and increased anxiety and worry.

Two and Three Year Old Children

In the twenty children between two and three years of age, behavior changes were reported. Although tantrums associated with increased independence is typical behavior, the tantrums were significantly greater than would be expected. Interactions between peers had to be mediated by staff at a higher frequency than prior to the bombing. This appeared to lessen approximately 8 months after the bombing. Both nap times and meal times were more difficult for the children and crying during these activities was not uncommon. The children were more demanding of staff for help with all activities. They were also more clingy to staff as well as to their parents. Regressive behaviors related to toileting, speech, and self-help skills were noted in a minority of children by both parents and staff members. Startle responses to noise and bright lights were seen, resulting in crying that was difficult to console. As media coverage of these surviving children was constant, requests to refrain from flash photography had to be issued.

Reenactments of the bombing were observed in these young children. For example, they built and crashed block towers. It was not uncommon for dolls to be thrown from play centers and left on the ground or picked up and "doctored." The children also focused on playing with rescue vehicles and costumes, particularly the firemen hats and police cars. This play continued throughout the year spent in the child-care center but tapered so that by the end of nine months, the children's play was not primarily related to the event. As with parents of the younger children, when questioned, many of the parents of these two and three year old children admitted to their own stress reactions related to the terrorist bombing.

Preschool Children

There were ten children between four and five years of age at the time of the bombing of the Murrah Federal building. With the relocation and the approach of summer, the number of children attending the daycare expanded. These more verbal children talked repeatedly about the bombing. They asked questions related to the building, fires, and rescue personnel. Children were often overheard comparing their scars or cuts or memories of these injuries and the bombing. Like the younger children, in the initial three months spent in the YMCA child care facility, the bombing-related play was the primary focus of their unstructured activities and it continued to diminishing degrees up to one year after the attack. Play appeared to center around two themes: the bombing and rescue activities. Building and crashing blocks was observed, complete with sound effects and narratives about the event. Early drawings included bombed buildings, fires, and hurt children. Many fire/police/ambulance toys were donated to the center in weeks following the attack. Children often fought with each other for use of these toys. Although superheroes such as Spiderman and Batman were still enjoyed, the children seemed to gravitate toward those toys that were involved in their rescue.

Behavioral changes were also noted in the older children. Like the younger children, nap times were more difficult than before the bombing. Children had more trouble falling asleep and were often observed to cry out in their sleep or sleep fitfully. They appeared more irritable with friends as well as with staff, with temper tantrums seen more readily. Although minimal, regressive behaviors related to self-help skills such as dressing and toileting were present. Staff and parents reported more clinging behaviors than prior to the bombing. Startle responses seemed more easily triggered than before the trauma. Shortly after the bombing, there were severe thunderstorms in Oklahoma City. Parents noted many of the children had difficulty with the loud noises and the lightening strikes. Again, flash photography was banned in coverage of stories related to these children.

Staff and parents caring for this age group were not immune from the event. They also reported some changes in their moods and sleep. The children's repeated questions and stories about the bombing, at times, was frustrating and anxiety-producing. Staff members working with this age group were observed to take more short breaks more than staff working with the younger children. It should be emphasized that these breaks were supported by administration and at no time were the children without adequate adult supervision.

Search and rescue teams including fire and police from across the country came to help in rescue and recovery efforts in the days and months following the bombing. Several of these teams visited the preschool children at the YMCA prior to returning to their homes. This proved to be beneficial for both the professional teams who found it gratifying to see young children who were survivors of the attack. The children asked many questions about the work of the teams and had the opportunity to tell their stories to the adults. The children expressed their appreciation with comments like, "Thanks for saving me from the bomb." Rescue play increased following the visits and the older children competed for the fire and police related toys.

INTERVENTIONS

In addition to observation, the mental health team provided psychoeducational intervention with both staff and parents. In separate sessions, staff and parents were provided information about common trauma responses in children. Suggestions for interventions were also provided. For example, assurances related to safety and security issues for the children were recommended. Touch (even a brief pat on the shoulder) was suggested as a way to assure the children of adult attention and presence. A return to a schedule and routine both at home and in the child-care setting was encouraged. The need for increased patience was emphasized and adults were instructed to provide help with activities that had previously been accomplished independently by the child. Praise and encouragement of success were stressed. Allowances for post-trauma play and drawing were also suggested. It was recommended that the center increase the number of rescue related toys available to the children in order to decrease conflict surrounding the use of these items by the children. Interwoven in these sessions was information related to how adults may respond to a trauma and normalization of many reported reactions to the bombing and its aftermath. The adults were advised about how the effects of their own irritability and mood swings may impact children. Suggestions for staff back-ups, buddies, and breaks as needed were made to increase the ability of the staff to continue to provide best care to the children while at the same time addressing some of their own needs. In order to maximize comprehension, this information was provided many different times over the course of the first six months. Individual discussions about children's behaviors were also available upon request by children.

The staff participated in a mandatory debriefing session, to process the bombing. Unlike the traditional debriefing of a single session (Mitchell, 1983), follow-up with small groups of staff and with individual staff members continued for two months. Weekly meetings were also available for parents to discuss the event and how they were managing its aftermath. Although most parents did not take advantage of these sessions, they expressed appreciation that they were available. Interestingly, many of the parents sought a team member for an informal "chat" as they dropped off or picked up their child from the center.

Unfortunately, no empirical data were collected related to the usefulness of the provided sessions. Qualitative information was obtained through interview. The majority of the staff and parents stated that it was reassuring to have the information. The discussions with the mental health team members also increased their confidence in their abilities to manage and help the children. They also reported it helped them feel better about their own reactions. More than once, parents and staff reported, "it is good to know I am not going crazy." Shortly after the mandatory staff meeting, staff members were individually asked about their perceptions of the meeting. Most of the nine staff reported that although they were wary of the mandatory meeting, it was extremely beneficial. They also noted that the follow-up discussions to the session were important as the single session brought many thoughts and feelings to the fore that needed to be further discussed. A minority of staff (two) stated that the session was difficult for them and they were continuing to have problems related to the bombing. It should be noted that, with rare exception, parents and staff did not pursue mental health services provided by the federally-funded programs after the bombing. It is unknown how the availability of other (non-grant-funded) mental health personnel impacted use of other services.

Interview Information and Posttraumatic Stress Symptoms of Parents and Children

Mothers of eleven children between the ages of one and six years (mean = 3.64, standard deviation = 1.57) were interviewed and evaluated for Post-Traumatic Stress Disorder symptoms approximately six months after the terrorist attack in Oklahoma City. Four of the children were male and seven were female. Most of the children were Caucasian (n = 9), with one African American child and one bi-racial child. In addition to being directly exposed to the event, many of the children were exposed via television coverage of the bombing. Parents reported that the average number of hours in the first week their children were exposed to this coverage was approximately eight (standard deviation = 8.86 with a range of 0 to 27 hours).

The parents were relatively close to the bombing site. The average distance from ground zero was 3.36 miles (standard deviation = 4.01). One parent was at the site. Most parents were reunited with their child in about 30 minutes, but some were separated for nearly two hours as they searched for their children. Parents reported greater media exposure in the first week after the bombing. Parents reported watching an average of 22 hours (standard deviation = 18.49) with a range of five to 60 hours.

Parental PTSD symptoms were assessed using the PTSD portion of the Structured Clinical Interview Diagnostic (SCID) (Spitzer, Williams, & Gibbons). These questions were also adapted for parental report of symptoms in the child. While the literature suggests that parents often underestimate child responses to a trauma, with the exception of post-traumatic play (R. S. Pynoos, personal communication, July, 1995), parental report was thought important as the majority of the children were preverbal or had limited language skills. The exposure criterion for PTSD, "exposure to a traumatic event or events in which a person experienced, witnessed, or was confronted with an event or events that involved actual of threatened death or serious injury, or a threat to the physical integrity of self or other" (American Psychiatric Association, DSM-IV, 1994) was met for both parents and children. Similarly, both parents and children responded to the incident with fear. All parents noted agitated behavior in their children and expressed their own feelings of horror and helplessness.

The second criterion of PTSD involves re-experiencing of the event. In young children this may be seen in their play. Frightening dreams without content related to the trauma also may be seen. Of the eleven parents, 8 met this criterion, but only three of the children were noted to have symptoms in this category. These children were slightly older. Interestingly, of the children observed by staff and the psychology team in the YMCA setting, all of the preschool children were showing post-traumatic play.

Another criterion of PTSD relates to "persistent avoidance of stimuli associated with the trauma and numbing of general responsiveness" (American Psychiatric Association, DSM-IV, 1994). This may be seen in efforts to avoid feelings or conversations related to the event as well as activities or people associated with it. Changes in mood and affect are also indicative of this criterion. Only one child was positive on this criterion, and five parents indicated positive responses.

A fourth PTSD criterion is persistent symptoms of arousal, including an exaggerated startle response. Seven parents endorsed these symptoms while they noted the arousal in only four of the children.

PTSD symptoms had been present for at least one month in the majority of parents and their children (n = 7 in both groups). The symptoms were not believed to be causing any significant impairment of functioning in any of the children and only endorsed by one parent.

Overall, no parent or child met criteria for a diagnosis of PTSD. Correlations between parental responses to the SCID and their responses for their child were not calculated due to the extremely small sample size. However, it is believed that one factor limiting a diagnosis of PTSD in the young child may have to do with the very fact that the child is young, thus resulting in an underestimation of the disorder. For example, verbal young children may not avoid conversations of the event, and may even be more likely to engage in repeated discussions and questions related to the trauma. Furthermore, as many of the criteria require an appraisal of internal feelings, preverbal and very young children may be unable to meet these (e.g., anhedonia, sense of a foreshortened future, feelings of detachment from others). A reexamination of criteria for application to the very young child appears to be warranted (Drell, Siegel, & Gaensabuer, 1993; Scheeringa et al., 1995).

Parents also completed a Parenting Stress Index (Abidin, 1990). The PSI total scores were clinically elevated (mean = 80.73, standard deviation = 16.84). Although the total stress score was high, no pattern was seen in subscale stress measures (e.g., child, parent, or parent-child domains). In general, parents were experiencing significant stress suggesting that more research is needed related to coping abilities and interventions to ameliorate the stress.

Additional Findings Related to Very Young Children

Brief on-sight intervention was also provided at a childcare program located at a center moved from ground zero. Similar to children in the YMCA, the preschool children repeatedly talked about the event and post-traumatic play was common. When provided opportunities to discuss the bombing, they readily accepted. Staff noted more irritability in the children as well as a change in sleep patterns after the bombing. However, unlike the children with greater exposure to the event, the behaviors in these children diminished more rapidly. Following a psychoeducational session with staff to discuss normal and common reactions to trauma in children (and adults), staff reported feeling more comfortable and confident in helping the children cope with the trauma than staff from the YMCA site.

Finally, supervisors and consultants from the Oklahoma Office of Child Care were provided with information about reactions to trauma. Guidelines for helping children were provided. Without exception, personnel stated that the information made their jobs easier. They were being asked to respond to many bombing-related questions and child behaviors by center and home based providers. Prior to obtaining the basic information, they reported feeling ill-equipped to provide satisfactory answers and hesitant to make suggestions.

CONCLUSION

In summary, very young children displayed reactions to a trauma that are not so different from those seen in more verbal children. Sleep disturbances and self-regulation issues appeared to be more problematic in infants than other age groups. Post-traumatic play and regressive behaviors appeared to be more common in toddlers and preschool aged children than in other age groups. Information to parents and childcare providers about reactions to trauma were reportedly the single greatest benefit for helping those caring for the youngest victims of a trauma. Similarly, repeated exposure to this information as well as opportunities to discuss their reactions seemed essential. Intensive individualized mental health services may not be the most efficient use of resources for young children and their caregivers. Indeed, very few children from the YMCA were referred for such services. Empirical research related to how psychoeducational information is utilized, impact on symptom expression and duration, interaction between parental/childcare provider reactions and child reactions and long-term reactions in the very young children is needed. This information may help triage care for this special population.

RISK AND MEDIATING FACTORS FOR PTS SYMPTOMS

There are certain factors that may increase a child's risk for development of PTSD after a trauma. One of these is injury from the event (Desivilya, Gal, & Ayalon, 1996; Pynoos & Eth, 1985), but witnessing the death or injury of others can also be a significant risk (Trappler & Friedman, 1996). The close relationship of a child to a victim can increase the risk of PTS symptoms (Elbidour et al., 1999). Indeed, the death of a child's parent or significant loved one due to a traumatic event, such as terrorism, can result in traumatic bereavement (Eth & Pynoos, 1994). Traumatic bereavement is the interaction of grief responses and trauma responses. When present, the PTS symptoms appear to complicate the child's ability to experience a grieving process (Goenjian et al., 1995; Pynoos, Steinberg, & Goenjian, 1996; Raphael & Martinek, 1997). Pynoos and his colleagues (1996) strongly recommend that the trauma and the grief be processed separately, with the trauma reactions needing to be addressed first before the grief can be effectively processed. It will be imperative to assess for this complicated type of grief in the thousands of children who lost relatives in the terrorist actions of September 11, 2001, and to develop interventions accordingly.

Parental reactions to a terrorist incident appear to impact how well a child will cope (Gurwitch et al., in press; La Greca, Silverman, Vernberg, & Prinstein, 1996). Similar findings have been obtained following natural disasters. After an earthquake, Pynoos and colleagues found that PTS symptoms were more likely if children appraised parental reactions as negative (Pynoos, Steinberg & Goenjian, 1998). Lyons (1987) has suggested that the best predictor of a positive outcome in a child is the ability of the significant adults in the child's life to cope with the event. While parental reactions appear to play a significant role, separation of the parent and child following a trauma is another important consideration. With separation comes an increased risk of exacerbated stress reactions and makes anxiety disorders more probable (Pynoos et al., 1998). With the disruption of transportation in New York City following the World Trade Center attacks, separation in families was undoubtedly extensive and possible lengthy. The impact of such separations in families is an important variable to assess. Prior functioning of the child as well as overall family stressors should also be considered. The more difficulties a child and/or a family has experienced prior to the trauma, the more likely the child is to develop PTS symptoms or related problems (LaGreca, Silverman & Wasserstein, 1998; Pynoos et al., 1998).

Based on data gathered after the Oklahoma City bombing, media coverage should be considered as a mediating variable for the development of PTS symptoms and related reactions. Coverage of the recent terrorist attacks in the United States was live and intensive; it continued for months. The war on terrorism fought around the world also has received extended coverage. Children across the country saw (and may continue to see) images of the events. Given this, it appears imperative to assess PTS symptoms not only in those children directly impacted by the events, but also those indirectly exposed through media coverage. It remains to be investigated if this finding is impacted by how coverage is viewed (alone or with others) as well as how it may be processed (e.g., discussion of images with caretakers).

The age of the child is a mediating variable in relation to trauma reactions (Green, Korol, Grace, Marshall, Leonard, Gleser, & Smitson-Cohen, 1991; Gurwitch et al., in press; Pynoos, Steinberg, & Wraith, 1995). Although there are similarities in how children respond to a trauma such as terrorist attack, children of different ages are also unique in their expression of processing the event. Without understanding how children may react, those trying to help children will be at a disadvantage as interventions should be developmentally appropriate (AACAP, 1998). For example, posttraumatic play is a common reaction in the young child, but is generally not observed in older children and adolescents. This reaction was reported to the senior author from child care providers not only in the areas directly impacted by the World Trade Center attacks, but also from providers working at a U.S. military base in Europe and others in cities across the United States. Following the September 11, 2001, attacks against the United States, a team of psychologists from the University of Oklahoma Health Sciences Center responded to a request from the American Psychological Association and the Oklahoma State Board of Education for a compilation (from empirical trauma and terrorist literature) of potential reactions in children; these were then posted on the agency's respected web sites. The reactions are summarized in Table 1.

Once typical childhood reactions and mediating variables are understood, interventions can be designed and implemented. Every child experiencing exposure to a terrorist event will not necessarily need intensive psychotherapy. Therefore, to determine allocation of resources and to better triage interventions, clinical needs assessments should be conducted (Gurwitch et al., in press). These assessments may effectively be conducted in the school settings (March, Amaya-Jackson, Murry, & Schultz, 1998). Ideas for psychological first aid as well as intervention approaches have been suggested by Pynoos and colleagues (Pynoos & Nader, 1988). In general, most experts support interventions which are trauma-focused (cf. AACAP, 1998; Berliner, 1997; Cohen, 1998; Gurwitch et al., in press). The efficacy of one model of brief intervention, Critical Incident Stress Debriefing (Mitchell, 1983), has been debated in the trauma literature (Foa, 2001). It was developed for use with adults. To apply such a controversial intervention with children without empirical support is of great concern (Cohen et al., 2000). More than one session of intervention is likely needed for children exposed to terrorism. Based on their review of trauma literature, Gurwitch and colleagues (in press) con-

TABLE 1. Possible Reactions in Children After Trauma/Disaster

- Worries, fears, and anxieties about safety of self and others (younger children may be more clingy to adults; older children may also have discomfort with these feelings of vulnerability)
- Worries about re-occurrence of violence (older children may also be worried about school violence and/or consequences of War on Terrorism)
- Changes in behavior
  - increased activity level
  - decreased concentration and/or attention (these behaviors may appear to be confused with ADHD in school-aged children)
  - angry outbursts or aggression (younger children may have increased temper tantrums)
  - increased irritability with friends, family, adults, and situations or events
  - withdrawal
- Changes in academic performance (usually a slight, short-lived decline) (adolecents may have an increase in absenteeism)
- Somatic complaints (e.g., headaches, stomachaches, vague aches and pains)
- Changes in sleep (young children may have nightmares seemingly unrelated to the trauma)
- Changes in appetite
- Decreased interest in usual pleasureable activities
- Increased negative behaviors (e.g., defiance) or emotions (e.g., sadness, anger, worry)
- Increased sensitivity to sounds (e.g., sirens, planes, thunder)
- Hate or intense anger statements (young children may show more hateful or hurtful play)
- Repeated questions or discussion of events (most common in young children) (young children may have posttraumatic play; school-aged children's comments may often be gruesome or graphic in nature)
- Preschool children to early elementary school children may show regressive behaviors (e.g., babytalk, bedwetting, tantrums)
- Late elementary through high school aged children may have a decreased sense of trust and more negative perceptions of others, particularly those perceived as "different." They may also have discomfort with feelings related to the perpetrators of the event, particularly revenge thoughts
- Older children may have repetitive thoughts about death and dying, including suicidal thoughts (by adolescents, this reaction may also result in an increase in risk taking behaviors such as alcohol and other substance abuse and promiscuous sexual behaviors)
- Some children may deny any impact of the traumatic event resulting in inappropriate comments, laughter, or rejection of those trying to process the incident

Adapted from R.H. Gurwitch, J.F. Silovsky, S. Shultz, M. Kees, & S. Burlingame. *Reactions and Guidelines for Children Following Trauma/Disaster (cf. www.helping.apa.org).*

cluded that essential elements of trauma-focused treatment include psychoeducation about trauma, cognitive coping skills and anxiety management, directly addressing the trauma, correcting misperceptions and misattributions, and components for parents/caregivers. The following are examples of some of the intervention programs for use with children.

One such program for trauma/grief focused work (primarily with adolescents) has been developed by the UCLA Trauma Psychiatry Program (Layne, Saltzman, & Pynoos, 2001). A variation of this program has been applied in post-war recovery with good results (Pynoos, Steinberg, & Goenjian, 1996). Based on work after the Oklahoma City bombing, a manualized treatment approach for use with young children (four through 12 years of age) was developed by Gurwitch and Messenbaugh (Gurwitch & Messenbaugh, 2001). The manual contains complimentary exercises for family involvement. In response to the events of September 11, 2001, La Greca and colleagues (2001) produced a manual for use with children (six through 12 years of age) and their families. Research examining the effectiveness of these treatments should be continued or investigated. Furthermore, as parents and caregivers are likely to underestimate children's reactions as well as effectiveness of treatment, multi-modal assessments and outcome evaluations are recommended (AACAP, 1998; Gurwitch et al., in press). Finally, the American Red Cross developed curriculum-based modules related to terrorism for use in school (Grades K-12) (American Red Cross, 2001).

Unlike other terrorist attacks against United States targets, the events of September 11, 2001, were not "static events'," but rather have been of a continuous nature. As recent as December 31, 2001 (CNN news, 12/31/01), a call for continued high alert against a terrorist attack through September 2, 2002 was reported. A CNN/Time Magazine news poll (*Time Magazine*, October 8, 2001) reported that 81% of adult respondents expected another act of terrorism in the next twelve months. When questioned about police preparedness for attacks, close to two-thirds of respondents believe that police are not able to adequately address such events. The ongoing governmental and citizen concerns are likely to create a heightened level of anxiety and stress in the both adults and children. Such ongoing events may lead to what Straker and the Sanctuaries Team (1987) have termed continuous traumatic stress syndrome.

This syndrome may be further exacerbated by the threat of attacks with invisible agents. In the CNN/Time poll (*Time Magazine*, 10/8/01), more than half of those polled believed that an attack with biological or chemical weapons was likely and nearly 25% believed a nuclear weapons attack, probable. Terrorism in the form of invisible agents seems more frightening than attacks by more conventional means (Becker, 2001). Fears of hidden and unknown dangers from these agents contribute to a heightened sense of vulnerability and feelings of uncertainty. Because of the strong concerns and fears, the potential for significant psychological impact is expected to be great (Holloway, Norwood, Fullerton, Engel, & Ursano, 1997; Simon, 1997).

As children are considered to be particularly vulnerable to invisible agent events, the Committee on Environmental Health and Committee on Infectious Diseases of the American Academy of Pediatrics (2000) reviewed concerns related to this population. The issues included greater risk of exposure to certain agents due to higher respiration rates in children as well as higher vapor density of some agents leading to fumes floating to children's breathing levels. The more permeable skin of newborns and young children coupled with greater surface-to-mass ratio will also increase exposure risk. The task force noted the increased potential of dehydration and shock if vomiting and diarrhea occur. Unfortunately, antidotes designed for use with adults are relatively unknown or contraindicated with young children. Although this report did acknowledge an increased risk for PTS symptoms in children with casualties or injuries, little attention was given to other psychological factors that may arise in the event of such attacks.

As in the case of conventional acts of terrorism, parental concerns about invisible agent attacks may impact their children. Philen and colleagues (Philen, Kilbourne, McKinley, & Parrish, 1989) noted that discussions of a possible invisible agent incident at a school coupled with media coverage of a possible event contributed to an outbreak of somatic complaints in school children. Parents of young children may be particularly vulnerable to PTS symptoms when concerns about invisible agent attacks exist. They evidenced increased anxiety and PTS symptoms with potential chemical and nuclear threats that occurred during the Persian Gulf War, Three Mile Island, and Chernobyl (Carmeli, Liberman, & Mevorach, 1991; Haavenar, Rumyantzeva, van den Brink, Poelijoe, van den Bout, van England, & Koeter, 1997; Bromet, E. J., Parkinson, & Dunn, 1990; Logue, Melich, & Hanson, 1981). Parents of young children may panic in their concern over their children's well-being. For example, following a radiological incident in Goiania, over 110,000 parents presented to an area hospital to have their children examined (Becker, 2001a). It is believed that no single hospital emergency department in the United States could effectively manage this number of "walking worried" at one time.

Parental fears and anxieties may also be expressed as anger which may intensify if trust in public officials and health care or government organizations is low (Becker, 2001b). This may be further heightened if parents perceive that care for their children is being withheld or distributed unfairly. Indeed, following the recent anthrax scares, newspapers, such as *USA Today*, contained stories of parents demanding vaccines for their children and becoming angry and accusatory of health care personnel for dismissing their concerns unjustly or with bias. Children's anxieties and fears may also exacerbate the situation in hospital settings as they may have negative associations with medical personnel and with illness-related treatments such as injections (Peterson & Mori, 1988). The situational fears, the cognitive capacity to understand what is happening, and the potential for negative reactions by parents may also significantly hinder the abilities of parents to manage their young children in the hospital setting. Henderson (1999) and Tucker (1997) have noted that there is increasing attention being paid to preparedness for bioterrorist incidents. Unfortunately, monies and attention to address the psychosocial impact on adults and particularly children has been relatively rare (Becker, 2001b). It is strongly recommended that these issues be given a higher priority in preparedness planning as the United States moves forward into a new era.

In examining current literature on terrorism and children, it appears that consequences may be significant and long-lasting. Not only are those children directly impacted by a terrorist act susceptible to PTS reactions and related difficulties, but so too are those removed from the event. Given the number of children across the United States who expressed their concerns and worries through cards, letters, and donations, it seems imperative that efforts to provide mental health resources to all in need be examined and made available. Although the expression of post-traumatic stress symptoms in the toddlers and children with early language is similar to those reported in older children (Drell, Siegel, & Gaensbauer, 1993), age-related differences exist. Furthermore, as reviewed in this article, reactions may be similar as well as different from adults. As mental health professionals begin to work with children, it seems important to reevaluate current standards of Post-Traumatic Stress Disorder as currently defined (AACAP, 1998; Scheeringa et al., 1995; Terr, 1985). In doing so, we may gain a more accurate picture of those children in greatest need of services.

The mental health needs of children must be a mental health and public health priority as the United States and countries around the world embark on a new page of history (Gurwitch et al., in press). The terrorist attacks of September 11, 2001 and its aftermath are likely to have long-range consequences for those children both directly and indirectly impacted by the events. Assessments followed by judicious and empirically guided interventions must be undertaken. Given that caregivers may mediate children's reactions to trauma, their involvement in any intervention seems extremely important (LaGreca, Silverman, & Wasserstein, 1998; Pynoos et al., 1998). In addition, novel mental health approaches, may also improve treatment outcome. For example, massage was used successfully with school-aged children following Hurricane Andrew (Field, Seligman, Scafidi, & Schanberg, 1996). More knowledge about children's responses to terrorism can be gained through partnerships between mental health, public health, medicine, and federal and private agencies. This knowledge can help guide long-range work in the area as well as address possible future events such as continued terrorist actions, invisible agent threat/attacks, and ongoing war. Hard as we try, it is not possible to completely shield our children from negative events. Only through continued education, service, and research efforts can we help those caring for children to meet the needs of our next generation.

REFERENCES

Abidin, R. (1990). *The Parenting stress index.* Charlottesville, VA: Pediatric Psychology Press.

Almqvist, K., & Brandell-Forsberg, M. (1997). Refugee children in Sweden: Post-traumatic stress disorder in Iranian preschool children exposed to organized violence. *Child Abuse and Neglect, 21*, 351-366.

American Academy of Child and Adolescent Psychiatry (AACP). (1998, October). Practice parameters for the assessment and treatment of children and adolescents with posttraumatic stress disorder. *Journal of the American Academy of Child and Adolescent Psychiatry, 37*(10), 4-26.

American Academy of Child and Adolescent Psychiatry (AACAP). (1998). Practice parameters for the assessment and treatment of children with posttraumatic stress disorder. *Journal of the American Academy of Child and Adolescent Psychiatry, 37*(10) Supplement, 4S-26S.

American Psychiatric Association. (1994). *Diagnostic and statistical manual of mental disorders* (4th ed.). Washington, DC: Author.

American Red Cross. (2001). *Facing Fear: Helping young people deal with terrorism and tragic events.*

Ayalon, O. (1983a). Coping with terrorism: The Israeli case. In D. Meichenbaum & M. Jaremko (Eds.), *Stress reduction and prevention* (pp. 293-340). New York: Plenum Press.

Ayalon, O. (1983b). Face to face with terrorists. In A. Cohen (Ed.), *Education as Encounter* (pp. 81-102). Haifa: University of Haifa Press.

Becker, S. M. (2001a). Psychosocial effects of radiation accidents. *Medical Management of Radiation Accidents* (2nd ed.) (pp. 519-525).

Becker, S.M. (2001b). *Enhancing preparedness for radiological terrorism incidents: Social, psychological and policy issues.* Oklahoma City, Oklahoma.

Berliner, L. (1997). Intervention with children who experience trauma. In D. Cicchetti & S. Toth (Eds.), *The effects of trauma and the developmental process* (pp. 491-514). New York: Wiley.

Bromet, E.J., Parkinson, D.K., & Dunn, L.O. (1990). Long-term mental health consequences of the accident at Three Mile Island. *International Journal of Mental Health, 19*, 48-60.

Carmeli, A., Liberman, N., & Mevorach, L. (1991). Anxiety-related somatic reactions during missile attacks. *Israel Journal of Medical Science.*

Cohen, J.A., & Workgroup on Quality Issues. (2000). Practice parameters for the assessment and treatment of children and adolescents with posttraumatic stress disorder. *Journal of the American Academy of Child and Adolescent Psychiatry, 37*(10), 4-26.

Committee on Environmental Health and Committee on Infectious Diseases, American Academy of Pediatrics. (2000). Chemical-biological terrorism and its impacts on children: A subject review. *Pediatrics, 3*, 662-670.

Desivilya, H., Gal, R., & Ayalon, O. (1996). Long-term effects of trauma in adolescence: Comparison between survivors of a terrorist attack and control counterparts. *Anxiety, Stress, and Coping, 9* (2), 1135-150.

Drell, M.J., Siegal, C.H., & Gauensbauer, T.J. (1993). Posttraumatic stress disorder. In *Handbook of Mental Health.* New York: Guilford.

Elbedour, S., Baker, A., Shalhoub-Kevorkian, N., Irwin, M., & Belmaker, R. (1999). Psychological responses in family members after the Hebron massacre. *Depression and Anxiety, 9*(1), 27-31.

Eth, S., & Pynoos, R.S. (1985). Developmental perspectives on psychic trauma in childhood (pp. 36-52). In C.R. Figley (Ed.), *Trauma assessments: A clinician's guide.* New York: Guilford.

Field, T., Seligman, S., Scafidi, F., & Schanberg, S. (1996). Alleviating posttraumatic stress in children following Hurricane Andrew. *Journal of Applied Developmental Psychology, 17*, 37-50.

Fields, R. (1982). Research on the victims of terrorism. In F. Ochberg & D. Soskis (Eds.), *Victims of terrorism* (pp. 137-171). Boulder: Westview.

Foa, E.B. (2001, November). *Early interventions for trauma: Possibilities and pitfalls.* Paper presented at the annual meeting of the Association for the Advancement of Behavior Therapy, Philadelphia, PA.

Goenjian, A.K., Pynoos, R. S., & Steinberg, A. M. (1995). Psychiatric comorbidity in children after the 1988 earthquake in Armenia. *Journal of the American Academy of Child and Adolescent Psychiatry, 34*, 1174-1184.

Gaensbauer, T.J. (1995). Trauma in the preverbal period: Symptoms, memories, and developmental impact. *The Psychoanalytic Study of the Child* (pp. 123-149). Yale University Press.

Green, B.L., Korol, M., Grace, M.C., Marshall, G.V., Leonard, C., Gleser, G.C., & Smitson-Cohen, S. (1991). Children and disaster: Age, gender, and parental effects on PTSD Symptoms. *Journal of the American Academy of Child and Adolescent Psychiatry, 30*(6), 945-951.

Gurwitch, R.H. (November, 2001). The impact of trauma and disasters on children. In S. Batten & M. Polusny (Chairs) *In the wake of terror: Science-based guidelines for mental health professionals.* Presented at the annual meeting of the Association for the Advancement of Behavior Therapy, Philadelphia, PA.

Gurwitch, R.H., Leftwich, M.J.T., Cote, M., Messenbaugh, A., & Pfefferbaum, B. (November, 1999). *Media impact on PTSD symptoms in young children following disasters.* J. Faust (Chair). Symposium on Models for Understanding Children's Reaction and Recovery to Diverse Traumas. Presented at the Meeting of International Society of Trauma Stress Studies, Miami, FL.

Gurwitch, R.H., Leftwich, M.J.T., & Messenbaugh, A. (August, 2001). *Posttraumatic stress reactions in young children.* In B. Pfefferbaum (Chair) Children and

Terriorism–The Impact of Bombings and Programmatic Responses. Presented at the annual meeting of the American Psychological Association, San Francisco, CA.

Gurwitch, R.H., Leftwich, M.J.T., Pfefferbaum, B., & Pynoos, R. (March, 2000). *The roles of age and gender on children's reactions to trauma and disaster: The Oklahoma City bombing*. Presented at the Third World Conference for the International Society for Traumatic Stress Studies, Melbourne, Australia.

Gurwitch, R.H., & Messenbaugh, A.K. (2001). *Healing after trauma skills: A manual for professionals, teachers, and families working with children after trauma/disaster.*

Gurwitch, R.H., Sitterle, K.S., Young, B.H., & Pfefferbaum, B. (in press). Helping children in the aftermath of terrorism. In A. LaGreca, W. Silverman, E. Vernberg, & M. Roberts (Eds.), *Helping children cope with disasters and terrorism: Integrating research and practice*. Washington, D.C.: American Psychological Association Press.

Gurwitch, R.H., Sullivan, M.A., & Long, P. (1998). The impact of trauma and disaster on young children. *Psychiatric Clinics of North America, 7,* 19-32.

Haavenaar, J.M., Rumyantzeva, G.M., van den Brink, W., Poelijoe, N.W., van den Bout, J., van Engeland, H., & Koeter, M.W.J. (1997). Long-term mental health effects of the Chernobyl disaster: An epidemiologic survey of two former Soviet regions. *American Journal of Psychiatry, 154*, 1605-1607.

Henderson, D.A. (1999). The looming threat of bio-terrorism. *Science, 283*(5406), 1279-1282.

Holloway, H.C., Norwood, A.E., Fullerton, C.S., Engel, C.C. Jr., & Ursano, R.J. (1997). The threat of biological weapons: Prophylaxis and mitigation of psychological and social consequences. *JAMA, 278* (5), 425-427.

Horowitz, M., Winler, N., & Alvarez, W. (1979). Impact of Event Scale: A measure of subjective stress. *Psychosomatic Medicine, 41*, 209-218.

La Greca, A.M., Sevin, S.W., & Sevin, E.L. (2001). *Helping America Cope: A guide to help parents and children cope with the September 11th terrorist attacks.* 7-Dippity Inc., Coral Gables, FL.

La Greca, A.M., Silverman, W.K., & Wasserstein, S.B. (1998). Children's predisaster functioning as a predictor of posttraumatic stress following Hurricane Andrew. *Journal of Consulting and Clinical Psychology, 66*(6), 883-892.

La Greca, A.M., Silverman, W.K., Vernberg, E.M., & Prinstein, M.J. (1996). Symptoms of posttraumatic stress in children after Hurricane Andrew: A prospective study. *Journal Consultation of Clinical Psychology, 64*, 712-723.

Layne, C.M., Saltzman, W.R., & Pynoos, R.S. (2001). *Trauma: Grief-focused group Psychotherapy program.* UCLA Trauma Psychiatry Service.

Logue, J.N., Melick, M.E., & Hansen, H. (1981). Research issues and directions in the epidemiology of health effects of disasters. *Epidemiologic Reviews, 3*, 140-162.

Lyons, J.A. (1987). Posttraumatic stress disorder in children and adolescents: A review of the literature. *Developmental and Behavioral Pediatrics, 8*, 349-356.

Macksoud, M., Dyregrov, A., & Raundalen, M. (1993). Traumatic war experiences and their effects on children. In B. Raphael & J.P. Wilson (Eds.), *International handbook of traumatic stress syndromes* (pp. 625-633). New York: Plenum Press.

March, J., Amaya-Jackson, L., Murry, M., & Schulte, A. (1998). Cognitive behavioral psychotherapy for children and adolescents with posttraumatic stress disorder following a single incident stressor. *Journal of the American Academy of Child and Adolescent Psychiatry, 37*(6), 585-593.

Mitchell, J.T. (1983). When disaster strikes: The critical incident stress debriefing process. *Journal of Emergency Medical Services, 8*, 36-39.

Nadar, K., Pynoos, R.S., Fairbanks, L., & Frederick, C. (1990). Children's posttraumatic stress disorder reactions one year after a sniper attack at their school. *American Journal of Psychiatry, 147*, 1526-1530.

Osofsky, J.D. (1997). Children and youth violence: An overview of the issues. In J.D. Osofsky (Ed.), *Children in a violent society* (pp. 3-31). New York: The Guilford Press.

Perry, B. (1997). *Childhood trauma and neurological and physical development.* Presented at the Oklahoma Department of Mental Health and Substance Abuse Services training Conference, Oklahoma City, OK.

Peterson, L.J., & Mori, L. (1988). Preparation for hospitalization. In D.K. Routh (Ed.), *Pediatric psychology* (pp. 460-491). New York: Guilford.

Pfefferbaum, B., Gurwitch, R.H., McDonald, N.B., Leftwich, M.J.T., Sconzo, G.M., Messenbaugh, A.K., & Shultz, R.A. (2000). Posttraumatic stress among young children after the death of a friend or acquaintance in a terrorist bombing. *Posttraumatic Services, 51*(3), 386-388.

Pfefferbaum, B., Nixon, S.J., Tucker, P.M., Tivis, R.D., Moore, V.L., Gurwitch, R.H., Pynoos, R.S., & Geis, H.K. (1999). Posttruamatic stress responses in bereaved children following the Oklahoma City bombing. *Journal of the American Academy of Child and Adolescent Psychiatry, 38*(11), 1372-1379.

Pfefferbaum, B., Nixon, S.J., Krug, R.S., Tivis, R.D., Moore, V.L., Brown, J.M., Pynoos, R.S., Foy, D., & Gurwitch, R.H. (1999). Clinical needs assessment of middle and high school students following the Oklahoma City bombing. *American Journal of Psychiatry, 156*(7), 1069-1074.

Philin, R.M., Kilbourne, E.M., McKinley, T.W., & Parrish, R.G. (1989). Mass sociogenic illness by proxy: Parentally reported epidemic in an elementary school. *Lancet, 2*, 1372-1376.

Pynoos, R.H., & Eth, S. (1985). Children traumatized by witnessing acts of personal violence: Homicide, rape or suicidal behavior. In S. Eth & R.S. Pynoos (Eds.) *Posttraumatic stress disorder in children* (pp. 17-44). Washington, DC: American Psychiatric Press.

Pynoos, R.H., & Nadar, K. (1988). Psychological first aid and treatment approach to children exposed to community violence: Research implications. *Journal of Traumatic Stress, 1*, 445-473.

Pynoos, R.S., Steinberg, A.M., & Goenjian, A.K.(1998). A public mental health approach to the postdisaster treatment of children and adolescents. *Child and Adolescent Clinics of North America, 7*(1), 95-210.

Pynoos, R.S., Steinberg, A.M., & Goenjian, A. (1996). Traumatic stress in children and adolescents: Recent trends and current controversies. In B. van der Kolk, A. McFarlane, & L. Wiesaeth (Eds.), *Traumatic stress: The effects of overwhelming experience on mind, body, and society* (pp. 331-358), New York: Guildford Publications, Inc.

Pynoos, R.S., Steinberg, A.M., & Wraith, R. (1995). *A developmental model of childhood traumatic stress.* In D. Cicchetti (Ed.), *Manual of developmental psychology, vol. 2: Risk, disorder, and adaptation* (pp. 72-95). New York: Wiley.

Raphael, B., & Martinek, N. (1997). Assessing traumatic bereavement and posttraumatic stress disorder. *Assessing Psychological Trauma and PTSD* (pp. 373-395). The Guilford Press.

Richards, C., Burstein, J., Waeckerle, J., & Hutson, H. (1999). Emergency physicians and biological terrorism. *Annals of Emergency Medicine, 34*(3), 183-190.

Scheeringa, M.S., Zeanah, C.H., Drell, M.J., & Larrieu, J.A. (1995). Two approaches to diagnosing posttraumatic stress disorder in infancy and early childhood. *Journal of American Academy of Child and Adolescent Psychiatry, 34*, 191-200.

Selden, B.S. (1989). Adolescent epidemic hysteria presenting a mass casualty, toxic exposure incident. *Annals of Emergency Medicine, 18*(8), 892-895.

Simon, J.D. (1997). Biological terrorism: Preparing to meet the threat. *JAMA.* 778(5), 428-430.

Sitterle, K.A., & Gurwitch, R.H. (1999). The terrorist bombing in Oklahoma City. In E.S. Zinner & M.B. Williams (Eds.), *When a community weeps: Case studies in group survivorship* (pp. 160-189). Ann Arbor: Taylor & Francis.

Small, G. W., & Borus, J. F. (1983). Outbreak of illness in a school chorus. *The New England Journal of Medicine, 308*(11), 632-635.

Small, G. W., Feinberg, D.T., Steinberg, D., & Collins, M.T. (1994). A sudden outbreak of illness suggestive of mass hysteria in schoolchildren. *Archives of Family Medicine, 3*, 711-716.

Swenson, C. & Klingman, A. (1993). Children and war. In C.F. Saylor (Ed.), *Children and disasters* (pp.137-163). New York: Plenum Press.

Straker, G. & the Sanctuaries Team. (1987). The continuous traumatic stress syndrome: The single therapeutic interview. *Psychology and Sociology, 8*, 48-56.

Taylor, B.W., & Werbickie, J.E. (1993). Pseudodisaster: A case of mass hysteria involving 19 schoolchildren. *Pediatric Emergency Care, 9*(4), 216-218.

Terr, L.C. (1985). Children traumatized in small groups. In W. Eth & R.S. Pynoos (Eds.), *Posttraumatic Stress Disorder in Children.* Washington, DC: American Psychiatric Press.

Time Magazine. October 8, 2001.

Trappler, B. & Friedman, S. (1996). Posttraumatic stress disorder in survivors of the Brooklyn Bridge shooting. *American Journal of Psychiatry, 153*, (5), 705-707.

Tucker, J.B. (1997). National health and medical services response to incidents of chemical and biological terrorism. *JAMA, 278*(5), 362-368.

Vogel, J.M., & Vernberg, E.M. (1993). Task Force report. Part 1: Children's psychological responses to disasters. *Journal of Clinical Child Psychology*, *22,* 464-484.

The Impact of Terrorism on Palestinians in Israel: An Interview with Eyad El-Sarraj

Eyad El-Sarraj
Lenore Meldrum

SUMMARY. Palestinian psychiatrist Eyad El-Sarraj, director of the Gaza Community Mental Health Programme, is interviewed by Australian psychologist Lenore Meldrum regarding the impact of terrorism on the Palestinian people. The differential effects of the loss of their homeland, the occupation, and the Intifada on various generations of the Palestinian community are discussed. A stable home and communicative mother are suggested to be stabilizing influences on the adjustment of Palestinian children in the midst of the violence in Israel. Valuation of the interests of the group over the individual, a tribal tradition that endorses revenge across generations, and the influence of extremist Islamic teachings are cited as forces that promote the practice of suicide bombing. The conflict in Israel is conceptualized as a cycle of violence between two communities that is only likely to be resolved through mutual respect by each faction for the humanity and rights of the other. *[Article copies available for a fee from The Haworth Document Delivery Service: 1-800-HAWORTH. E-mail address: <getinfo@haworthpressinc.com> Website: <http://www.HaworthPress.com> © 2002 by The Haworth Press, Inc. All rights reserved.]*

Eyad El-Sarraj, MD, is affiliated with Gaza Community Mental Health Programme.
Lenore Meldrum, is affiliated with the University of Queensland.
Address correspondence to: Lenore Meldrum, BEd-BPsych, MMedScience, P.O. Box 198, Kenilworth, Queensland 4574 Australia (E-mail: Lenore. Meldrum@mailbox.uq. edu.au).

[Haworth co-indexing entry note]: "The Impact of Terrorism on Palestinians in Israel: An Interview with Eyad El-Sarraj." El-Sarraj, Eyad, and Lenore Meldrum. Co-published simultaneously in *Journal of Trauma Practice*. (The Haworth Maltreatment & Trauma Press, an imprint of The Haworth Press, Inc.) Vol. 1, No. 3/4, 2002, pp. 125-132; and: *Trauma Practice in the Wake of September 11, 2001* (ed: Steven N. Gold, and Jan Faust) The Haworth Maltreatment & Trauma Press, an imprint of The Haworth Press, Inc., 2002, pp. 125-132. Single or multiple copies of this article are available for a fee from The Haworth Document Delivery Service [1-800-HAWORTH, 9:00 a.m. - 5:00 p.m. (EST). E-mail address: getinfo@haworthpressinc.com].

KEYWORDS. Palestinian, Gaza Community Mental Health Programme, terrorism, loss, homeland, occupation, Intifada, adjustment, Israel, violence, tribal tradition, revenge, extremist Islam, suicide bombing, humanity, rights

Although one often encounters accounts in the news media of Palestinian terrorists, many Palestinians living in Israel also consider themselves to be victims of acts of terrorism by the government of Israel. In order to better understand their viewpoint and experiences, Australian psychologist Lenore Meldrum interviewed Palestinian psychiatrist Eyad El-Sarraj about the impact that the violent conflict in Israel has had on the psychological adjustment of the Palestinian people. The interview was conducted via telephone on January 11, 2002.

Dr. El-Sarraj was born in Beersheva, Palestine, and studied medicine in Alexandria University in Egypt and psychiatry at the Maudsley Hospital in London University. When he first arrived in Gaza, he was the only psychiatrist in the region. In 1990 he founded the Gaza Community Mental Health Programme, where he recruited and trained a staff that now numbers 220. In addition to his work in mental health, he is also known for his contributions in the area of human rights. He directs the Independent Commission for Human Rights in Palestine, is a member of the International Rehabilitation Centre for Torture Victims and of the Co-ordinating Committee of the Campaign Against Torture Victims, and he was winner of the 1998 Martin Ennals Award for Human Rights Defenders.

Lenore Meldrum, BEd-BPsych, MMedSc, graduated from James Cook University of North Queensland with a joint degree in Education and Psychology and Master of Medical Science awarded by the University of Queensland. She was employed as a Researcher with the Department of Psychiatry, the University of Queensland prior to taking up appointment with the Queensland Health Department. She recently retired as the Research and Evaluation Psychologist at the Integrated Mental Health Service, Royal Brisbane Hospital District, but has retained her long-standing links with the Department of Psychiatry, The University of Queensland as an investigator in a National Health and Medical Research funded research grant. Previously, she has been involved in planning, conducting and evaluating training programs for mental health professionals in Government services, in private practice, and for members of the business community in Australia and New Zealand, she is currently President of the Australasian Critical Incident Stress Association, and Editor of their journal *Forum.*

LM: Tell me a little about yourself, your profession, your current position, and basically how you came to be working where you are today?

ES: I am the director of the Gaza Community Mental Health Programme. I am a psychiatrist by profession. I am the director and the founder of the Programme, which was founded in 1990. I studied medicine in Alexandria University in Egypt and studied psychiatry at the Maudsley Hospital in London University.

LM: What was it like for you having been the only mental health professional in the Gaza Strip when you first arrived there, especially in the midst of such pressing need for services? When you arrived there and saw the intense need that was there and you were just one person?

ES: Yeah that's right.

LM: How did you feel sort of facing that sort of intense need?

ES: I came back to Gaza in 1978. And then I was the only psychiatrist for the Gaza Strip, which had a population of nearly 1 million people. And at the time I felt that I was doing or trying to do something that is worthwhile because of the humane needs for counseling, particularly when it comes to children. So, I was always proud of that. I was doing a kind of duty as a psychiatrist as somebody who had the privilege of being educated when other people were not. And I was only repaying my debt to the people of the land. So I was always happy to function here and to do work. And when I was dismissed from my job as a psychiatrist in the public health department, by the Israeli occupational authorities, I started the Gaza Community Mental Health Programme, which is a non-governmental organization, in 1990. And I'm much more gratified than rewarded now because I had the chance then to open the way for psychologists and social workers and nurses and other professions to be trained in the area of mental health and community services. Today I am happy to say that we have 220 people working in the Gaza Community Mental Health Programme. So, so far it's been very gratifying.

LM: A colleague of mine working with survivors of the Port Arthur shootings here in Australia found that three generations of one family who were victims of the shooting displayed very different reactions to that event. Could you comment on what effect terrorism has had on the different generations of Palestinian people? Specifically say on senior members of your community, the young adults, the adolescents and the children?

ES: Yes. Well, you see you have to consider two important aspects here, which is the political history of the area and social history. In the last century, in the last 53 years the Palestinians have had severe repeated forms of torment. It started in 1948. Senior members that I'm thinking of were adults then. It started in 1948 with the expulsion and the uprooting of Palestinians, who became refugees. And living in refugee camps that has led to a kind of inner focus of pain and fear of losing suddenly the house by force and not being able to go back, has continued to be the most important single event in psychological mechanisms that affects the Palestinians across generations. This is why today when the Israeli forces destroy a house for the Palestinian community it is the most brutal and the most violent form of punishment.

LM: Because they're losing their homes all over again?

ES: Exactly, because of the repeated trauma. Because it makes them relive the original trauma of expulsion and uprooting. And the reaction of the Palestinians is very intense indeed.

LM: Is it different though for the different generations? The adolescents now, are their reactions different now from say those people who were some of the refugees in 1948?

ES: Yes, this is actually different for people for instance who are from that generation of 1948. They continue to dream, literally dream, of return, of going back to their homes, to their villages in Palestine. I have once seen a case of senile dementia, which was a man of, you know, old age, which his memories, recollections stopped at 1948. Everything, everything that happened after 1948 was not there. And the reality of what happened before 1948 are memories of very emotional detail.

LM: Yes. Very, very, strongly encoded by the sound of it.

ES: Yes. Exactly. And this man was caught when he was old a few times leaving his home in Gaza refugee camp where he lives now, where he used to live–he's dead now–and going, walking to his original town which is now part of Israel in Jaffa. And he was brought back by the Israeli police a few times from Jaffa. And when they found him in Jaffa these times he was always in his original house.

LM: But it's those early memories that are so strong and that really seems to keep them going. Now some research, particularly some here in Australia, has shown that exposure to traumatic events has been linked to an increase in violence in the home.

ES: Yes.

LM: Do you believe there's any evidence of that link as exposure to interpersonal violence in the form of terrorism to any increases in violence in the home in the way of abuse and that type of thing?

ES: Absolutely. We found out, you know we started in 1990 in the Gaza Community Mental Health Programme to deal with the children of the Intafada. "Children of the Stone" as we call them, the children who are in the forefront of the throwing stones at the Israeli soldiers. And we concentrated on helping these children and trying to guide them while involved in fighting–of violent acts, even throwing stones. At the same time, trying to counsel the children and their families for the effects of trauma. But very quickly we discovered there is an intense emotion of anger, of resentment and of violence, which was directed against the children. And we found out that a great majority of the fathers of these children were in Israeli prisons during interrogations. Let me just finish putting the picture for you. In 1967 Israel occupied the West Bank and Gaza and the Palestinians who are already refugees, and in 1987, late '87, the Palestinian Intafada started, which was mainly a spontaneous popular uprising of stones against the Israeli solders. But quickly it was overtaken by militant Palestinians with arms and in combat with the Israeli soldiers and they started then the suicide bombing inside Israel, which has killed Israeli civilians. That was a form of terrorism the Israelis were subjected to and in retaliation Israel started to use different methods of punishment of destroying neighborhoods and of people and torture. This cycle of violence of Palestinians and Israelis who are severely traumatized and who are dominated by extreme national sentiments and religious sentiments. So that today both populations of Palestinian and Israelis are squeezed between the two extreme elements in their societies.

LM: How do you think the development, both emotional and cognitive, has been affected in the children and adolescents who've actively participated in the Intafada?

ES: Well you see we found out in, during the work we do here that Palestinian children become politically aware very early on in their time. So a child of three and four years old is playing a game called "Arabs and Jews." And that is a very interesting game to watch and observe the behavior of the children, because a few years ago Palestinian children, some of them, were preferring to play the role of the Jew, the Israeli. For them, the Israeli is a person of power and then always children at that age like to identify with power. To do it now, many of these children play the role of the Palestinian suicide bomber or the martyr as they call them. For them, this martyr represents power. So you can, from this game you can observe that development of that political awareness of children at a very early age.

LM: Has it impeded their cognitive ability, their ability to learn?

ES: Yeah. There's a study done by a French organization called Terre Des Hommes and they found out that 15% of the children under the age of 15 in Gaza are suffering from a kind of lag in physical and intellectual development due to chronic malnutrition and chronic trauma. And then we found out that one of the most common symptoms of trauma and violence is the diminished concentration of children and lack of scholastic achievement.

LM: Yes, it's sad, isn't it?

ES: It's not only because of the trauma but also because the classes are overcrowded and the teachers themselves are traumatized.

LM: That's I think one of the things that most Australians feel the strongest about, is the impact that it has on children because they seem to lose their childhood. What can we learn from the Palestinian people about how to cope with that ongoing threat? Is there a safe way, a healthier way of coping with the threat of terrorism? Or, do you feel that it may well overwhelm the people?

ES: Well, I tell you today that almost every single person in Gaza today is traumatized to one degree or the other. I am dealing in my own house with my father who is 85 years old and with my little niece who is three years old and between them, different generations, and each and every one is showing signs of trauma to one or another degree. In the last month, we have been subjected to waves of F-16 bombing of Gaza, which was so horrible and terrifying. And what we have learned about effects of trauma and coping are two things. One is, mother is the most important figure and the most important symbol of stability, continuity, and warmth–that the presence of mother is the most important single factor of protection. The other factor is the house. As long as the house is intact, people continue to be able to cope.

LM: So this is the difference between the people who cope well and those who require a lot of professional intervention?

ES: Absolutely. Now mothers who are there and communicating with the children have better children in terms of psychological make-up than families who don't have mothers or mothers who will not communicate with the children.

LM: Can you say something about this martyrdom that the children now see with the suicide bombers and that sort of thing? Can you explain that, psychologically, in the context of the social and cultural forces that facilitate that practice in your country?

ES: Yes. One thing is that the Palestinian people are still tribal people. This means in this particular setting that they identify with the groups and the individual is sacrificed for the group. Second, they are very much in their tribal tradition that they are requested to take revenge across generations. And the people here have also become victims of extremists teaching of Islam. Islam, as all forms of religions, is a big and complex book, which can be interpreted in so many ways. The tribal identity, the Islamic teaching, which is extreme, the original trauma of the Palestinians–all these are linked to the new phenomenon of the martyrs or suicide bombers.

LM: One thing that I'm interested in as a professional who has taught self-care for a long time–how do you care for yourself and how has it affected your view of human nature?

ES: Well, I came to believe very much that the Palestinian-Israeli conflict is essentially a conflict between two kinds of victims. Jews, who have been victimized by persecution and discrimination and the Holocaust in Europe and in their attempt to address their history in the form of Israel. They have helped hurt the Palestinians because essentially the establishment of Israel was at the expense of the Palestinians who became the new victim. And I believe that there is only one way in which the Israeli-Palestinian conflict can be addressed and can lead to peace–only if this picture is understood by the two sides. The victimization and the cycle of violence between the two communities has led me to believe that only respect of humanity and human rights is the key to resolution for any conflict–if the people, particularly the political leaders are aware of the deep psychological impact of the conflict in the two communities. I have been part of the Palestinian delegation to the peace talks with the Israelis and I was armed with my knowledge of the cycle of violence in trying to bridge the gap between the two sides and I believe I was able to help in that respect. That has for me meant also a form of coping with my own victimization by using my experience to help to reach peace. I also believe strongly that there is a God in every child–Jewish, Muslim, or Christian–and no one has the right to kill that God, particularly in the name of God. I go for long walks. I have a group of friends who form together a support group. We continue to talk and express our traumas and feelings of pain in the support group. And all throughout the years I was helped by these groups.

LM: That's wonderful, to have such a group that you can unload to I think is so necessary for all professionals in this field. Well, I'd like to thank you sir very much for your time. I have no other questions. Is there anything that you feel that I haven't asked you that you would like to express in this interview?

ES: I just want to conclude by praying that we one day will have peace and justice in the Holy Land, which sometimes seems like it is being taken by the Devil.

LM: Thank you very much, sir. I do hope that some time you may come and visit us in Australia.

ES: It would be my pleasure and I'd be honored.

LM: Thank you sir for your time.

ES: Thank you.

The Impact of Terrorism on Jews in Israel: An Interview with Ofra Ayalon

Ofra Ayalon
Frances S. Waters

SUMMARY. In searching for information on the effects of living with the ongoing threat of terrorism, Israel was an obvious place to turn. For several years now reports of acts of terrorism and violence occurring in Israel have appeared in the news media as frequently as several times a week. Moreover, one of the more common types of terrorist acts regularly taking place there, suicide bombing, coincides with the method used in the September 11th attacks in the U.S. The impact of ongoing terrorism on children and their families has been an area of expertise of Israeli psychologist Ofra Ayalon for many years now. Dr. Ayalon was interviewed by Frances S. Waters, a clinical social worker and licensed marriage and family therapist in independent practice in Marquette, Michigan. The interview was conducted via telephone on January 12, 2002. *[Article copies available for a fee from The Haworth Document Delivery Service: 1-800-HAWORTH. E-mail address: <getinfo@haworthpressinc.com> Website: <http://www.HaworthPress.com> © 2002 by The Haworth Press, Inc. All rights reserved.]*

Ofra Ayalon, PhD, is affiliated with Nord International Trauma Consultancy, Tivon, Israel.

Frances S. Waters, MSW, LMFT, is in Independent Practice, Marquette, Michigan.

Address correspondence to: Frances S. Waters, MSW, LMFT, 706 Chippewa Square, # 205A, Marquette, MI 49855 (E-mail: Fswaters@aol.com).

[Haworth co-indexing entry note]: "The Impact of Terrorism on Jews in Israel: An Interview with Ofra Ayalon." Ayalon, Ofra, and Frances S. Waters. Co-published simultaneously in *Journal of Trauma Practice* (The Haworth Maltreatment & Trauma Press, an imprint of The Haworth Press, Inc.) Vol. 1, No. (3/4), 2002, pp. 133-154; and: *Trauma Practice in the Wake of September 11, 2001* (ed: Steven N. Gold, and Jan Faust) The Haworth Maltreatment & Trauma Press, an imprint of The Haworth Press, Inc., 2002, pp. 133-154. Single or multiple copies of this article are available for a fee from The Haworth Document Delivery Service [1-800-HAWORTH, 9:00 a.m. - 5:00 p.m. (EST). E-mail address: getinfo@haworthpressinc.com].

KEYWORDS. Terrorism, Israel, violence, trauma, interpersonal violence, family, political violence, attacks, impact, intervention, adults, children, threat, psychosocial programs, traumatic effects

Ofra Ayalon, PhD, is an internationally renowned traumatologist with a lengthy career as a leader, educator, author, and trainer in the field of terrorism. She was a senior lecturer for 35 years at the University of Haifa, and currently is the director of Nord International Trauma Consultancy, and senior consultant at the Community Stress Prevention Center in Kiriat Shmona-Tel Hai College, Israel. Her career as a trainer and consultant has spanned every continent and many notable organizations, such as UNICEF in Yugoslavia, Finland's Red Cross, Center for Crisis Management & Education in England, Aoibashi Family Clinic in Japan, Somprasong Royal Educational Organization in Thailand, and the Basic Family Therapy Training in Istanbul's Bakish Center. She has conducted extensive, longitudinal research on the impact of domestic violence, trauma, stress, major disasters, war terrorism, and bereavement on children and their families.

Frances S. Waters, MSW, LMFT, a clinical social worker and licensed marriage and family therapist, has specialized in the field of child abuse for 30 years. An internationally recognized educator, trainer, consultant, and clinician in the area of childhood trauma and dissociation, she has presented nationally and internationally in this field. She regularly conducts forensic evaluations and is an expert witness in child abuse cases. She served on the Executive Council of The International Society for the Study of Dissociation (ISSD), and is currently on the Scientific and Professional Advisory Board of The Leadership Council for Mental Health, Justice & the Media. She has published four chapters in *The Dissociative Child: Diagnosis, Treatment & Case Management*, and several articles on childhood dissociation.

FW: I'm excited to learn more about your perspective on terrorism. Have you been writing on this subject?

OA: Oh yes. I've been writing for over 25 years on this subject. As a matter of fact, I am writing right now quite a few commissioned chapters and articles for the United States. So, I'm busy doing this now.

FW: Are there some particular writings that you would like to note at this time that you're working on?

OA: I am writing now about three phases of disaster intervention: before, during, and after the event. I will mention my research, teaching, and clinical work as we go along. If you need to know something specific about this, just ask me.

FW: Can you describe the different forms of terrorism that have occurred in Israel over the years?

OA: Much to my regret, I have experienced a great variety of this kind of violence. I will start with the form of terrorism against Israeli citizens that was quite common in the 1970s and 1980s, the taking and killing of hostages. I will mention a few events that involved children. As a traumatologist, I deal with the whole community, but my focus is always on the more vulnerable populations, and children are the most vulnerable. A very traumatic event, which is known as "the Ma'alot Massacre," happened in 1974 when 105 teenagers, who were camping overnight in a school away from home, were held up by three terrorists and kept as hostages for fourteen hours. Just a few managed to escape. While the event was going on, the whole country held their breath, because no one knew what was going to happen and how it was going to end. It ended in a bloodbath, as the terrorists, who killed 22 children and wounded 56, were killed by the Israeli rescue squads. I started making contact with the survivors in hospital immediately afterwards and continued meeting them and observing their progress for over 20 years. So I gained not only long lasting contact with quite a few of them, but also the possibility for a longitudinal perspective of what really happens to survivors and their families. A few years later, a major attack was launched on a large group of families on a weekend outing. Two buses were hijacked and 38 people were killed, a lot of them members of the same family.

Another tragic hostage taking happened in a northern small seaside town named Nahariyah. A father and his five-year-old daughter were taken from their beds as hostages and then brutally murdered by terrorists. At that time terrorist attacks happened every few weeks. The most traumatic feature of these cases, apart from the carnage–the killing and the wounding–was the prolonged period when the victims were face to face with the perpetrators. This created for the survivors additional stress–the proximity, the close eye contact. Different exchanges that happened between these two groups, the perpetrators and the victims, affected the survivors for a long time in the aftermath. Just imagine what happens when a stranger smiles in the face of a five-year-old girl and shoots her in the belly at the same time. This dissonance creates for the survivor a tremendous difficulty in the ability to ever trust another human being.

Later we experienced terrorist attack in the form of drive-by shootings, which is a form of violence not unfamiliar in American cities. When I visited trauma units in American hospitals, I saw both the perpetrators and the victims of drive-by shootings lying down in the same room.

Yet another form of terrorism, which is very vicious and quite frightening, is the hiding of explosives in ordinary articles–such as bags, watermelons, etc. Innocent looking articles left on the streets, for example, a loaf of bread, a small refrigerator, a little toy, a scooter motorcycle, and letterboxes. These are loaded with explosives and are turned on by remote control in the most crowded places. So, in Israel, if you leave your bag somewhere in a crowded place, the chances are that nobody will take it, but police will be alerted immediately, because the fear of booby traps is so great–greater than the urge to possess something that doesn't belong to you.

A typical method of attack on civilian populations has been the shooting of rockets from over the border. As you are familiar with the geography of Israel, it is a very small country. It's really difficult to conceive just how tiny it is, not bigger than New Jersey perhaps. It is surrounded with borders on three sides, except for the sea. For those who choose to terrorize our country, it's quite easy to shoot at residential areas from across the border. And recently we are under perpetual terrorist attack from the Palestinian authority attacking us from within the border. We are all in the shooting range of almost every shooting gun or rocket. Since the 1970's, rockets from Lebanon have been targeting the northern town of Kiryat Shmona, This Israeli border town was for years under fire, and again children were especially targeted in schools and kindergartens. As a matter of fact, that is where I started my professional work on trauma and there is where our Community Stress Prevention Center was established in 1980. Since then I developed the C.O.P.E. method for stress management and for developing coping skills. This program has been implemented in the entire school system in Israel and then translated to several languages and used in war and terror stricken areas such as Former-Yugoslavia and North Ireland.

Another form of terrorism experienced in Israel has been attacks on school children. School children seem to be targeted a lot. For example, last year a class of 12-year-old girls from a religious school were visiting, quite symbolically, the Valley of Peace on the Jordanian border. All of a sudden, seven girls were shot dead in their backs in front of all the others. That happened on a school trip that was intended to portray the spirit of conciliation and peace.

For the last few years we became familiar with suicide bombers who blow themselves up in crowded places such as buses, shopping malls, and restaurants. Our unfortunate experience with dealing with victims of this atrocity brought me to America in September 2001. I was sent on a joint mission of the Ministry of Foreign Affairs and Jewish Federation to different American cities to explain to the media and other audiences how the Israeli society has been coping with suicide bombings. The interesting point was that in the first week of September this particular subject did not trigger much interest, but then the 9/11 attack on America happened and the atmosphere changed completely. Everybody became very interested to hear how we have been coping and many American psychologists have been consulting with me since then on that issue. I hope I answered your question on different types of terrorist attacks.

FW: Can you talk about the effects of terrorism on the population as a whole, and then the effects of terrorism on special populations, for example, the Holocaust survivors and their children?

OA: It's very well known that the aim of terrorism is not just the number of casualties. It is the infliction of fear and unpredictable impending danger. As a matter of fact, terrorism is meant to demoralize the population, although it doesn't always succeed in doing that. The aim of terrorism is to win the psychological war. So, terrorism is like a killing machine in many ways, but its main aims are psychological and political. Politically, it is trying to extort something from a third party, such as a government, by using random people as pawns. This method can only work against societies that place a high value on human life. It never works in a country where there is no reverence for individual lives. It can't work against a culture that enlists young people and promises them sexual and other gains in heaven if they sacrifice their lives by killing others, either for political or religious purposes. And then, there is no wonder that the terrorists target the most precious groups, which usually are the children. In every society, children are the most vulnerable and most valued group. That is especially true in a society of survivors, who live under the shadow of the Holocaust. In the Israeli society children have a very special place, not only in the hearts of their parents, which is self-evident, but also in the community as a whole. Children are the future. Children are the proof that the Holocaust genocide is not going on and that there is hope for a national resurrection. So when children are targeted, it's most painful. In that area terrorism is very successful in hurting us, because a lot of the targeted victims, not only casual victims, are children.

FW: So they're trying to impact on the future political arena of Israel by attacking the children who would in the future have some impact, as well as to continue to demoralize your country. Is that correct?

OA: I can't say what is their explicit intention. Terrorism doesn't have an explicit agenda. It must be the implicit aims of terrorism, as you see from the fact that they target kindergartens or schools or school children on an outing or school buses. Many buses came under fire when it was obvious that these were school buses with small children.

FW: Yes.

OA: My sense is that the Palestinians know that this is the most painful form of terrorism. Children can't talk for themselves; they can't protect themselves; they can't understand. It's very painful to lose a child that way.

You asked what are the threats inflicted by terrorism? There are a number of threats that disrupt daily life. First, it's an on going threat to life. It can happen everywhere. People would say, "Oh, I'm going on the train, who knows if I'm coming back alive?" Sometimes people say it as a kind of black humor. But beneath the humor there is this impending fear that any train or bus can become a death trap.

Another area is the threat to bodily integrity. It refers to the danger of losing your health and becoming crippled, which is the plight of a great many survivors of terrorists' attacks. A lot of these people suffer terrible pain and remain handicapped and crippled. Yet another source of threat is the dread of losing our dear ones, our beloved, spouses, dearest friends. Young people fear for their parents. Parents always say, "I fear for my children." I heard people say, "A child's pain or injury is even worse than my own pain. I wish it would have happened to me instead of my child."

An additional threat involved in terrorism is the threat to homes and the general feeling that your home is not your castle, as terrorists burst into homes and kill people in their beds. During the Gulf War in 1991, in which Israel did not even take part, over 2,000 homes were hit by the rockets sent from Iraq. On top of the rocket bombings, the whole population was under threat of chemical warfare. For 40 days and nights we had to wear gas masks and sit in sealed rooms during each attack. The fact that 2,000 homes were actually hit by such a long-range missile was very disconcerting.

Terrorism also imposes a threat to our value system. My belief is that human beings live by values. Certain values can be different from each other, but we all need some value system. For example, one of the basic values that we seldom stop to question is: "Can we trust another human being?" We know that the world is not a particularly safe place, but we put much emphasis on "attachment" in early age, and try to instill in babies and small children a sense of "basic trust." And why do we do this? Because we know that this is the psychological foundation for a healthy being. Without trust you can't even put one leg in front of the other and walk through life. As I told you before, when you come face-to-face with terrorists' viciousness, you get in touch with something so destructive in the other person that it destroys this basic trust. So, there is a very great danger to one's own value system. When trust in other human beings turns to be misleading, then any stranger is potentially perceived as an enemy. This is one damaging outcome of perpetual encounters with terror. Fran, as a therapist you surely know that as human beings we are all struggling with aggressive drives. We have innate aggression, as a part of our need to survive as a species in the world. But culture and education try to tame or channel our aggression. We don't want to eradicate aggression altogether, but we want to channel it so it becomes an energy resource, like electricity, for example. It can become a positive energy that pushes us forward to learn to defend ourselves. But, confrontation with so much destructive aggression on the other side may break the fragile acquired psychological defenses against lashing out. This process is especially dangerous for children, because in a paradoxical way, the terrorists may become their role models.

FW: Yes, because they have power.

OA: And it's not true only in our case, but this is an analysis of the threat of terrorism all over the world. Aggression breeds aggression.

FW: Do you see, through the accumulation, the multigenerational transmission of violence and traumatic experiences?

OA: I do. In dealing with the aftermath of terrorism, one of the questions is: "Who needs help?" It is well known that traumatic experiences trigger traumatic responses. To explain who needs help I'll use a metaphor of a pond full of frogs. When a stone is thrown into the pond, it kills the frogs that are directly hit. But then, what happens to all of the other frogs? They are caught in the ripples and suffer from shock. This is the ripple effect of fear and anxiety. When a terrorist attack hits and kills its victims, the eyewitnesses are also victimized. Families who lost their dear ones, friends, peers, are all victimized. And so are the rescue workers who come in close contact with the horrors of death and injury. Those "circles of vulnerability" also include the medical staff, social workers, teachers, and psychologists who are exposed vicariously to the trauma of their students and clients. A lot of them are hidden victims, who carry hidden scars. Often they themselves don't realize how wounded they are. They are often neglected by post trauma health services as well. The usual response to an eyewitness who shows signs of shock is, "What do you have to complain about? Look at you. Nothing happened to you. Go play. Go pray. Leave me alone. Don't bother me." Following recent trauma research, we don't think so any longer. We know now that eyewitnesses go through very similar traumatic experiences as the victims themselves.

FW: And how is that?

OA: There is a psychological process described as a "near miss" experience. A near miss victim is someone who feels: "I could have been there. It could have happened to me." When the media brings the events in full-blown colors and sounds to every home, we all become eyewitnesses, in spite of ourselves. When people watch reported destruction and killing on TV, it can draw them into the circle of "near miss." The "circles of vulnerability" include people who are close to the victims or survivors, like family and friends, colleagues and peers, classmates of a child who's been hurt or injured. Very seldom would school authorities stop to think that these children need help, as much as the "real" victims. But then, the whole peer group needs some help. The "near miss" is troubled by fear and guilt: "I could have been there. Why him? Why was she on the bus? I didn't go on this tour or this trip. If I were, it would have happened to me and not to my best friend." Whenever children are hit, the same age kids all over the country may identify with them and become agitated. Remember the seven girls who were shot in the Valley of Peace? They were 7th grade students. Children of the same grade all over Israel were very troubled. "Wow, this is our grade. We could have gone to the Valley of Peace. We could have become the victims that day." And others bargain: "Oh no. Our route would be different. We would have gone along the beach." Thus the circles of vulnerability are expanding. . .

FW: Now, what about the caregiver?

OA: We have to consider the primary rescue workers, those who collect the bodies and the limbs from the street–and then the doctors and the medical rescue crews, the ambulance teams, and the fire brigades. Even they are not immune. They just learn how to hide a lot of what's going on inside and keep a stiff upper lip, and may suffer from burnout. There is also some other factor that helps them. There are psychological gains and benefits from being active and doing something useful. When you can actually do something, have some role, it is empowering. Then we have to remember that the psychosocial caregivers are vulnerable too, even though they are also empowered by their roles. So there is a very delicate balance here. We also have to think about the clergy, the social workers, the teachers, and us psychologists who need to contain the survivors' pain and a lot of it rubs on us.

FW: Now, what are the exacerbating factors of people's stress? Who will be more vulnerable than others?

OA: The exacerbating factors would be the extent of the severity of the plight. In case of a severe injury or permanent handicap the trauma lingers on. Then the geographical proximity to the event and the psychological and social proximity to the victims might be additional factors. People who had endured previous loss or trauma– especially those whose trauma went unattended. For example, when we deal with victims or survivors of recent terrorist attacks, some children in the classroom would burst into tears. And you would wonder why, but then you'll find out that this child lost a mother when she was two years old, or that this boy's parents were divorced and he didn't see his father for a whole year. So, there are hidden wounds that usually go unnoticed and they open up in such cases.

FW: They get triggered or surface?

OA: They get triggered and reopened and need a great deal of care. Social support has been found to be the major factor in healing. Support can come from family members, teachers, peers, or people who belong to a "shared fate group." Sometimes we conduct groups of people who suffered similar events in their lives, but not necessarily at the same time, who support each other.

FW: What else helps?

OA: Activity is an important factor. Grown-ups find their own way to become active, but children don't. They are expected to go on being dependent on adults, going to school, doing the routine things. We learned over the last half-century how to prepare children of all ages even from kindergarten age to deal with trauma and allow them to become active either in a metaphoric or symbolic way, or by helping others in some altruistic manner. Thus, they become empowered. As you know, if you can help anybody who's a bit less able than you, you become much stronger no matter what happened to you at the same time. It's a human trait and we are using this in our intervention programs.

FW: What helps besides being active?

OA: Another element that is very helpful in coping with stress is having a belief system. We found out that people with religious beliefs usually cope better. They can pray. They can pray and believe that there is somebody looking over them, that some higher power is really taking care. It doesn't matter which faith and how you worship God, as long as one has the belief that there is a bigger power than oneself. But there are other ways of having faith and developing a belief system. One of them is having a sense of trust. When you look at Holocaust survivors, you may wish to know whether they are more vulnerable or less vulnerable than others. Some are actually more vulnerable, because their wounds never healed. They may be living under the shadow of catastrophic expectations. When disaster strikes they may say, "Oh, I knew that my life was only given back to me for a short time and now it's going to be taken away, or my dear ones are going to be hurt as I expected." Others with similar backgrounds may feel that once they have survived the most horrible experience, they are immune in some way. They are resilient. And they empower themselves with this belief. Depending on your belief system, you can turn the event from a disaster into a challenge. Look how children cope–children learn to be resourceful. But they can also learn to be helpless. Past experiences are responsible both for learned helplessness as well as for learned resourcefulness. But psychologists, counselors, teachers, and parents can turn the tables. We can use activities and interventions to turn learned helplessness into learned resourcefulness. If we leave it to the individual child, we never know what's going to come out.

FW: Could you talk about imagination and anger?

OA: All right. What is the role of the imagination in coping? It is a double-edged sword. One can harbor rescue fantasies, even while enduring the most horrible hardship, and this may be empowering. But then imagination can produce catastrophic images, even when nothing awful happens, and this weakens the resilience. Psychological research hasn't found out what affects this difference in the use of imagination. I cannot really explain why one would develop rescue fantasies and another will develop catastrophic expectations. But I know from my research and my clinical work that this makes a whole lot of a difference in resilience and coping with stress.

FW: Do you think that parents play a role in whether they–

OA: Oh yes. Parents supply modeling, especially for young children, who experience the world through the parents' eyes. They also provide a sense of security. Parents' anxiety affects their children.

Another response to terroristic trauma is anger. Anger can be an energizer and can be put to good use. It is important to feel angry and to be able to vent anger and not feel guilty, although our society has very little tolerance for anger. Women are even less allowed to be angry than the men. Anger can be healing, but rage, hostility, and revenge can blindfold the person and dissipate the energy. So you see how these coping mechanisms are polarized? Anger can be healing in certain circumstances when it is channeled in a right way, accepted and not repressed. But if hostility, rage, and revenge become obsessive, they dissipate the energy and can be very destructive.

I have described some short-term responses. But you also wanted to know what the long-term effects are.

FW: Yes, the long-term effects on children.

OA: The effects on children and on the family are connected with the type of intervention offered to them after a terrorist attack. Sometimes the intervention is planned and sometimes it's spontaneous. Either way, communication and expression of feelings is of utmost importance. It is expressed in the quote from Shakespeare's play *Macbeth*: "Give sorrow words. The grief that does not speak–whispers o'er-fraught heart and bids it break." This is ancient wisdom, before psychology became so popular and academic. We encourage people to express themselves when they are in misery. But it's not enough to encourage communication, because we don't communicate in a vacuum. We need validation and acceptance. But this is easier said than done. It's very difficult to listen and listen with compassion to all this pain. We try to shun away from listening to other people's pain. The greatest challenge in the long-term intervention is to develop a positive self-image, to *turn from victim to victor!* We are not trying merely to survive, but find the inner courage and feel that "I've done it, I can live with the pain, and I can live with the loss. They haven't broken us." I hear this many times in debriefing sessions. If you can help somebody to get to this place, from victim to victor, it's a good intervention. There certainly is growth from trauma.

FW: I'd like to know what strategic interventions you recommend to assist children.

OA: This is my most favorite topic. It brings out my life work over the last 25 years or more. I've been engaged mostly in devising new methods of intervention, especially for the school system. My coping programs have been implemented in the school system in Israel but also in translation in countries, like Thailand, Finland, Japan or Turkey. During the war in former Yugoslavia, my team and I trained local psychologists to help the victimized communities in all 5 warring countries. My book on coping has been translated into Croatian and has been used in refugee camps and schools. Its Spanish translation was in demand in Argentina after the Jewish community building was bombed by terrorists and there were many victims.

FW: What is the name of the book?

OA: It is called *Rescue: Community Oriented Preventive Education.* These four words create the acronym C.O.P.E. The program was written originally in Hebrew and then I used the English translation in Ireland, England, and the United States. It has been translated into a few other languages I don't even speak. There are parts translated into Arabic sitting on my desk, and hopefully it will be used to help the Palestinian population that is badly traumatized as well. I really hope that this brings some sort of solace to children all over the world. I feel that if I made any contribution, it is by approaching, researching and writing about trauma interventions and teaching it worldwide. If you wish, I will elaborate on just a few features of this program. Ok?

FW: Yes, excellent.

OA: The most recommended short-range crisis intervention is called "debriefing," developed by Dr. Jeffrey Mitchell mainly for disaster rescue workers. Basically, it means that people who have been involved in traumatic events need to have an opportunity to talk and process their experience right afterwards and preferably in small groups. It's better to do this in a group rather than individually, to share and normalize traumatic reactions and get support from the group. When survivors seek individual consultation, they may be stigmatized as weak or abnormal. A debriefing is not a clinical model but a psychosocial model of psychological first-aid. It is also a method for triage–screening high-risk individuals who may need more help. I use my own adaptation, called "debriefing for empowerment," developed in collaboration with the American psychiatrist Dr. David Soskis. We ask: "What did you feel, think, and do during the event that was helpful to you? What did you feel, think, and do during the event that was unhelpful to you? What did others do that was either helpful or unhelpful?" Survivors and helpers alike find these questions empowering. Debriefing is also a very good screening device, especially when large numbers of people are involved. After the debriefing, you can narrow down the amount of people who you would recommend for further help.

FW: Now, in the triage, who are involved? Who comprises the triage?

OA: We employ various professionals such as social workers, psychologists, teachers, or counselors trained in debriefing. Sometimes we train doctors as well. Different people from different professional venues can become facilitators for debriefing, depending on the situation, if you are in the desert, or in the middle of the battlefield, or in a hospital. Deriefing does not follow a medical/pathological model. Rather, we emphasize "that everyone reacts a bit abnormally to an abnormal situation, and this is normal." This is the official APA's (American Psychiatric Association) definition of traumatic responses. So, it's an abnormal response to abnormal situations, which is normal.

Now, how do we know who is the high-risk person who will need more help? Who would be the more vulnerable survivor? Those who are bereaved and injured will need a more personalized and prolonged intervention. And those who suffered previous disastrous life events that make them vulnerable even when they don't realize that themselves, for example, immigrants. Israel is a country of immigrants and so is the United States. Immigrants are people who have gone through lots of loss–loss of language, loss of country, loss of home. Even in the case of voluntary immigration, not necessarily refugees, they are struggling with a lot of traumatic loss. When a new trauma occurs, it may shake the very fragile ground they're treading on. When we deal with trauma we need to be very sensitive to immigrants, especially when they don't really understand the cultural and social codes, and they don't know where to turn for help. You know, they really are on a strange planet. It doesn't matter if they arrived in the country two weeks or three years earlier, if they think they are strangers, they feel like strangers.

Lonely and isolated people, the aged and estranged teenagers are vulnerable. They may develop Post-Traumatic Stress Disorder (PTSD). They may have phobic reactions, recurrent nightmares, intrusive memories, and projected anger. They are totally shaken in many ways and the symptoms don't tend to go away. In order to curb the symptoms and not to allow the situation to become chronic, they will need specialized help.

FW: I was wondering if there's a link between exposure to interpersonal violence such as the Holocaust and terrorism, and violence in the home in the form of partner-battering and child abuse?

OA: First and second generation Holocaust survivors comprise a large part of the Israeli society. Not everybody would automatically need help. But in special support groups, they confess that present terrorist attacks trigger past horrors. You also wanted to know how exposure to terrorist violence affects the family and if we have more domestic violence and child abuse.

I can use my own research and clinical experience dealing with domestic violence as a family therapist. I've written two books on the subject of child abuse and domestic violence and another book on divorce. There is no evidence at all that there is a connection between the external and the family violence, though we see a growing number of cases of psychological, physical, and sexual abuse of children, and wife battering. There is a lot of violence in our society and a lot of traumatization, but we couldn't establish a research connection. There is a lot of overprotection in families of Holocaust survivors. On the whole, the Israeli family is closely knit and bonded.

Terrorism is not the only element influencing growth in Israel. It's one of the elements but not the most prominent, not the most dominant. Let me give you an example: A very interesting research looked at two similar small towns, a border town that suffered from shelling and terrorism, and the other of similar social-economic structure, a relatively quiet central place. Children's dreams of these two towns were compared and no outstanding differences were found. There were nightmares both here and there and also other kinds of dreams here and there, but nothing to indicate that children who were more exposed were more destructive or anxious than others. And why is that? One equalizing factor can be the fact that it is a small country, where everybody is similarly affected by the same disasters. Whether you come under fire or you only see the attacks on TV, or your friends or your cousins are there, you already are part of the circle of vulnerability. It doesn't matter where you live. And the other factor is the resilience developed over time by living in such a dangerous environment.

FW: Would numbing be an explanation?

OA: I don't think that you can call it numbing, though there is a lot of escapism, healthy escapism, but not numbing, not callousness, I would say. Not that adults or children don't feel anything–this would be numbing–but that they divert their attention to different things. They divert their energy into play and imagination. Young people, for example, when they finish their army service, take off for a year or more to track and backpack in wild places in South America or Africa, as if [jokingly] they are looking for more trouble it seems, and sometimes they get into real trouble. But this is of their own choice. They are taking control over their lives. It may be this is a kind of escapism. The fact is that we don't have more people or children in trouble in those parts of Israel that suffer more from terrorism than in other parts. Another interesting example of the connection between terrorism and attitudes comes from longitudinal research on the kids who were rescued from the traumatic hostage situation in their teens. We conducted a follow up over twenty years, until they were 37, with families and all. Their political choices between right and left wing was very similar to the general population. They were not more extreme than their non-traumatized age-group.

FW: How do you explain that?

OA: This is my perspective–that terrorism and war are not the only elements that shape life in Israel, though if you look at the screen on TV, the BBC and CNN, that's the only thing you see. It's a small fraction of our lives.

FW: What other elements do you think have a profound impact on a child's ability to cope with this constant threat of safety as a result of terrorism?

OA: First and foremost, there is the family influence. Family in Israel is very cohesive. Families keep together, three generations, four generations. They see each other often. They eat together on weekends. They meet on the holidays and they are on the phone every day. We have something that you can call the 'mobile phone mania." Every child now goes to kindergarten with a mobile phone. Why?

"Mommy wants to know what you're doing now, dear." Parents say, "Yes, I'm quieter if I know exactly what happens," because of the threat of terrorism. But there is also a trend in this, a bit overprotective, suffocating kind of family, which in certain situations is a buffer against trauma. You don't want it day in and day out, you know. But when the situation is not safe, it's nice to know that somebody cares.

FW: There's that sense of constant connection then with their parents, that they're close to their parents in spite of the perhaps impending danger around them.

OA: Yes. And there is open communication between generations on most political and other issues. I remember once when I was teaching family therapy in Kyoto, I had a big audience on family issues in Israel. In Japan, they don't communicate freely across gender and generations. Children and parents are not intimate. Husbands and wives don't share much, practical matters only, but not heart to heart talk. When I told them that in Israel people always talk to each other in the family, share their feelings and political ideas, share their knowledge and their history, the Japanese students found it difficult to believe. They said, "It cannot happen in a family." But you know, it does happen.

FW: Well Ofra, do you think that is one of the main buffers in helping children?

OA: No doubt. Family is a very important buffer against stress. But I must tell you that there is also a high level of anxiety in family members. And because children pick up the anxiety from their parents, it's the responsibility of the parents who are stressed to deal with their own anxiety and try not to transmit it to the children. We pay a lot of attention to that concern, by running lots of parents' guidance groups in Israel. But I'm sure that many children do absorb their parents' stress and anxiety. So, it's a mixed bag. Sometimes the family bond even increases anxiety. But, as a whole, family is a place to go to and if parents succeed in maintaining stability and safety at home, they succeed in instilling hope in their children. This helps. For example, people say to their children–I heard this from my parents and my children heard it from me–"Oh, you wouldn't believe how much harder it was in the old times." [jokingly] So, all right, it was harder and you're still around. This means you are very strong indeed!

FW: Let me just ask you, before we get to reconciliation, is there anything more you would like to say about strategic interventions to help children?

OA: If I may, I will talk to you a little bit about methods of crisis intervention and enhancing resilience and coping in children. Okay?

FW: Yes, excellent.

OA: First, we do think that children are resilient, but still they need help to become better copers. I mean not only Israeli children. Children are resilient because otherwise there would be no children left in the world. You know, the state of the world is not so great. So, children are resilient by nature and they can really cope with adversities, with a cost of course, but they do. We believe that it is our responsibility to enhance their coping resources. So, we have built a special holistic model of enhancing coping skills. The model is made of separate educational modules. Our model, co-created with my colleague Dr. Mooli Lahad, is called "BASIC-Ph." Each of these letters stands for one channel of coping that we identify and enhance through specific activities. "B" stands for Belief. The program would promote positive affirmation of resilience, for example, values, search for meaning, or religious beliefs, if that is the case. We use metaphors in stories and poetry, also Bible stories, to develop the spiritual appraisal of our human situation in the world. And this would be appropriate in America and any other country, depending on the value system of the society. The importance of value systems is very high in enhancing coping.

"A" stands for Affect–feelings and emotions. A great number of stories and activities help children identify and express their feelings. But this would also be true if I trained doctors or if I trained media people. It would serve to enrich the "feeling vocabulary." It would be more important for people who come from Mars than for people who come from Venus, you know? And of course, you can see the reason why–women can talk a lot more about their emotions than men. Men usually don't even have the words for it. And children, boys and girls, don't have a rich enough vocabulary for feelings. These activities enhance their "emotional intelligence," by helping them identify a wide range of feelings and express them non-verbally by drawing, drama, music, movement, and verbally by talking of course, using metaphors, stories, and creative writing. Whenever I teach traumatology in different cultures I use a special brand of therapeutic story-telling cards, that are universally valid, in order to enhance the ability to identify and to express feelings.

The "S" stands for the Social coping channel. First, we reinforce the group process and give good modeling. The facilitators become role models. They reinforce the group's dynamics, group sharing and support. We know that for a child to have a role in the group and also to be able to share experience is very empowering. So, there are many activities involved in the social channel. We use the power of the group, for example, for simulations. To create a simulation you need people to assume roles and to practice problem solving and value clarification you need to have a group. So the group is actually the unit through which we develop the individual's coping skills.

The letter "I" represents imagination. A lot of emphasis is put on working with imagination because it's the source of creativity, and coping is about finding alternative ways of surviving. When you are sitting in a sealed room or in an air raid shelter for hours and days, to have an imaginary friend or to be able to enter fantastic reality of "as if" games is the utmost coping skill. Only imagination can help you fly and divert attention from the danger at hand. Humor is part of imagination. Using humor is healing and therapeutic.

"C" stands for the cognitive channel. Gathering reliable information helps to cope with uncertainty. We suggest telling children the truth.

Though not to overburden them with truth needlessly. Don't tell them everything, but tell them as much as they need to know. Never lie, never gloss over the reality. They're going to find out and lose trust in you. If you need to talk to children about death, talk to children about death. They can take it. It's also important to curb the "rumor industry" by giving reliable information. Children can learn how to solve problems; they also have their own ideas of how to do it. Ranking the order of priorities when for instance, a child loses a house in a fire or sustains another loss nobody knows where to begin to pick up their lives. Cognitively you can help people rank the order of priorities, rearrange their personal story of this disaster to tell it again and again until they get this story to where they are a victor and not a victim.

"Ph" stands for the Physical coping channel. Because stress is connected with brain activity, we teach how to detect psychobiological cues of extreme stress and teach relaxation to reduce stress. C.O.P.E. includes a package of relaxation and physical activity exercises for children. We also teach nutrition for stress reduction.

I hope I gave you some ideas how the BASIC Ph model works. It is important to notice that all the activities such as story-making, guided imagery exercises, and simulations are presented with clear instructions for the facilitator, but they are open ended for the users. The participants can take it to wherever they need to. So, it's a combination of a teaching and therapeutic method.

FW: I'm impressed with the comprehensive, multi-faceted aspects of your approach and helping a child in many, many different ways of processing the traumatic experience, and using the groups to do that must be very valuable.

OA: Thank you, Fran. Most existing intervention programs for children are mainly cognitive. Our special contribution is this comprehensive holistic view that taps all the different resources in different people. These methods have been developed and employed by the very creative team of psychologists in the Israeli Community Stress Prevention Center.

FW: Yes. And Ofra, it's very similar to the kind of work I do with children as well in bringing all of the mind-body, the social-cognitive- emotional aspects together. Now, I could go on for a long time hearing you, but we should probably get to the last question on reconciliation. Can you speak about the concept of reconciliation and peaceful resolutions that can help countries mend their differences and minimize the breeding ground for future terrorism?

OA: This is like opening a "Pandora's Box." Hopefully at the bottom of the box we may find hope. I will share with you a psychological view of reconciliation, not a social or political view. I don't want to minimize the importance of all these aspects. But on the psychological level, I learned from Jungian theory that we project our denied aspects of personality onto others and try to destroy the other as a way of getting rid of what we hate in ourselves, which is unknown to us. The way to reduce conflict is to deal with the enemy within, to acknowledge these aspects of ourselves. It seems a long way removed from solving an old and bloody political conflict, but there is no conciliation without this self-awareness.

FW: I agree. I agree. I think that it's our shadow self that we haven't come to terms with that we do project onto others in trying to resolve it. Now, how can you use your wisdom to teach us in the United States to cope with terrorism?

OA: You will never catch me in such a patronizing attitude of pretending to know more than my colleagues in other countries. I can only share what I have learned from my life experience with terrorism. When the attack on America happened it caught me in the middle of my media tour on terrorism. I came to New York and went as close as I could to Ground Zero and spoke to a lot of people in Manhattan. I realized their need to find new ways to confront the horror of the situation. Since then I have been commissioned to write and consult a few U.S. organizations and colleagues. What I learned from them was that American society is less cohesive and much less knit together, which is both good and bad. On one hand, it reduces the circles of vulnerability. On the other hand, it reduces the circles of support. Fewer people feel hurt, but fewer people are there to offer support. I noticed this as I went from Canal Street to uptown New York, there were less pictures of the victims and much less flags, as if it was a different place. People looked differently, less shocked maybe, and this was just two or three days after the attack. I hear from many of my American colleagues that there is some reluctance to be involved in trauma prevention and preparation for future terrorist attacks. I know that there is a lot of military prevention, security prevention, but not so much in education and psychology. There is healthy denial that helps carry on with life, but it also leaves the population vulnerable and unprotected from whatever may happen. The next time over may be more painful than the first time, because it creates re-traumatization. It's more difficult to cope if we don't attend to the initial trauma. My suggestion is that it would be worthwhile to implement psychosocial prevention in the educational system. This was done, for example, in former Yugoslavia after the war, because trauma didn't end with the ending of war. Our team trained psychologists and psychosocial agents to start programs in schools, so children can both work through past events and also replenish their coping resources for future eventualities. If American schools would allow time and resources to implement into the curriculum programs such as C.O.P.E. or similar programs, it would be for the benefit of the younger generation, and hence for the whole society. A comprehensive psychosocial preventive curricula will deal with children's past trauma and at the same time develop new coping skills. If I could contribute in any way to this future, using the experience accumulated over the years, I would feel gratified. It is sad that we need a blow to wake up, but we usually grow from a blow, and this is the time for growth.

FW: Yes, Ofra, so well said. I just can't tell you how much I immensely appreciated the opportunity to do this interview and how much I have learned from you today. And I admire your work greatly and I'm hoping that we in America can listen to your words and carry forth on what you know so well in your country that we're just really beginning to learn in our country about terrorism. And it's just been a pleasure, Ofra. Thank you so much.

OA: At this point I wanted to tell you that you asked wonderful questions about how terrorism affected growing up in Israeli society. I'm sure that if we'd have a panel of nine or more, they will each describe their different views. Some of the things I have told you come from research–mine and others–but on the whole I gave you my own perspective, of a woman psychologist, born in pre-state Israel before the Second World War and who raised two generations in Israel. Thank you, Fran. Thank you for listening. Thank you for being interested.

FW: Oh, absolutely.

REFERENCES

Ayalon, O. (1982). Children as hostages. *The Practitioner, 226*, 1771-1773.

Ayalon, O., & Soskis, D. (1986). Survivors of terrorist victimization. In Milgram (Ed.), *Stress and coping in time of war* (pp. 257-274). Brunner/Mazel: New York.

Ayalon, O. (1987). Living in dangerous environments. In M. Brassard, R. Germain, & S. Hart (Eds.), *Psychological maltreatment of children and youth* (pp.171-182). New York: Pergamon Press.

Ayalon, O. (1988). Children as hostages: Vulnerability and resilience. In E. J. Anthony & C. Chiland (Eds.), *The child in his family, vol. 8: Perilous development: Child raising and identity formation understress* (pp. 443-456). New York: John Wiley & Sons.

Ayalon, O. (1993) Post traumatic stress recovery. In J. Wilson & B. Raphael (Eds.), *International handbook of traumatic stress syndromes* (pp. 855- 866). New York: Plenum Press.

Ayalon, O. (1998). Community healing for children traumatized by war. *International Review of Psychiatry, 10,* 224-233.

Ayalon, O. (1992). *Rescue!: Community oriented preventive education for coping with stress.* Ellicott City: Chevron Publishing.

Ayalon, O. (1993). Post traumatic stress recovery. In J. Wilson & B. Raphael (Eds.), *International handbook of traumatic stress syndromes* (pp. 855-866). New York: Plenum Press.

Ayalon, O. (1998b). Reconciliation: Changing the face of the enemy. In O. Ayalon, M. Lahad, & Cohen (Eds.), *Community stress prevention 3* (pp. 62-69). Jerusalem, Ministry of Education & Kiriat Shemona: C.S.P.C.

Cognitive Processing Therapy for PTSD in a Survivor of the World Trade Center Bombing: A Case Study

JoAnn Difede
David Eskra

SUMMARY. The present case study describes the successful treatment, including long-term follow-up of a survivor of the first World Trade Center (WTC) bombing who developed posttraumatic stress disorder (PTSD). The literature indicates that behavioral, particularly exposure based techniques, and cognitive applications have shown promising results in reducing symptoms of PTSD, in adults exposed to combat and rape. To our knowledge, no treatment protocol has been developed for PTSD following a terrorist incident. This paper presented the application of a PTSD treatment protocol based on Cognitive Processing Therapy (CPT) (Resick & Schnicke, 1992, 1993) in the treatment of an adult female exposed to such terrorist trauma.

JoAnn Difede, PhD and David Eskra, PhD, are affiliated with The New York Presbyterian Hospital-Weill Cornell Medical Center.

Address correspondence to: JoAnn Difede, PhD, The New York Hospital-Cornell Medical Center, 525 East 68th Street, Box 200, New York, New York 10021 (E-mail: jdifede@mail.med.cornell).

[Haworth co-indexing entry note]: "Cognitive Procesing Therapy for PTSD in a Survivor of the World Trade Center Bombing: A Case Study." Difede, JoAnn, and David Eskra. Co-published simultaneously in *Journal of Trauma Practice* (The Haworth Maltreatment & Trauma Press, an imprint of The Haworth Press, Inc.) Vol. 1, No. 3/4, 2002, pp. 155-165; and: *Trauma Practice in the Wake of September 11, 2001* (ed: Steven N. Gold, and Jan Faust) The Haworth Maltreatment & Trauma Press, an imprint of The Haworth Press, Inc., 2002, pp. 155-165. Single or multiple copies of this article are available for a fee from The Haworth Document Delivery Service [1-800-HAWORTH, 9:00 a.m. - 5:00 p.m. (EST). E-mail address: getinfo@haworthpressinc.com].

KEYWORDS. Treatment, World Trade Center, WTC, post-traumatic stress disorder, PTSD, symptoms, adults, combat, rape, terrorist, Cognitive Processing Therapy, CPT

INTRODUCTION

The present case study describes the successful treatment and long-term follow-up of a survivor of the first (February 26, 1993) World Trade Center (WTC) bombing who developed posttraumatic stress disorder (PTSD). Recent reviews of psychotherapy and pharmacological treatment outcomes (Solomon, Gerrity, & Muff, 1992; Shalev, Bonne, & Eth, 1996) suggest that behavioral, particularly exposure based techniques, and cognitive treatments have shown promising results in reducing symptoms of PTSD, primarily in veterans and victims of sexual assault. To our knowledge, no treatment protocol has been developed for PTSD following a terrorist incident. In the present case, Cognitive Processing Therapy (CPT) (Resick & Schnicke, 1992, 1993), an intervention which has proven effective for the treatment of PTSD following sexual and criminal assault, and which incorporates both exposure and cognitive techniques, was adapted for the treatment of PTSD in a survivor of the WTC bombing.

CASE REPORT

Assessment Method

K. was evaluated using the Structured Clinical Interview for the DSM III-R (SCID; Spitzer, Williams, & Gibbons, 1987) and two well-validated, widely used, self-report instruments, the PTSD Symptoms Scale (PSS) (Foa, Riggs, Dancu, & Rothbaum, 1993) and the Brief Symptom Inventory (BSI) (Derogatis & Melisaratos, 1983). The instruments were administered at several time points: seven weeks after the incident as part of an assessment study of survivors of the WTC (Difede, Apfeldorf, Cloitre, Speilman, & Perry, 1997); pre-and post-treatment; one-year; and then again, two and one-half years after the incident.

Seven Weeks Post-Trauma

K., a single woman in her early thirties, was near the epicenter of the WTC explosion when the bomb was detonated. During her evaluation she described with little emotion being blown into the air and landing on her arm, which was badly broken. She attempted to make light of her experience trying to engage the interviewer, as if she were recounting an amusing story. K. noted, with effortful humor, how she was "blown out of her shoes."

K.'s articulate, energetic presentation was consonant with her position of significant authority in a large corporation. Although glimpses of her engaging and energetic personality emerged throughout the interview, she became more tearful and frightened as she elaborated on how the bombing, and her injury, had affected her life. K. described feeling vulnerable and having difficulty coping with the demands of her job since the bombing. She stated that she could not concentrate and that she felt guilty about her job performance. About six months prior to the bombing, she had changed jobs. She was still getting settled in her new position when she was injured and she felt that she owed the company for the resources that they had invested in her professional development. Although K. returned to work two weeks after the blast, she found that she became very anxious riding the subway, and so, began to work from home. Shortly thereafter she determined, with the advice of her corporation's consulting physician, that the demands of her rehabilitation prevented her from working at all. So, she obtained temporary disability.

K. was diagnosed with PTSD using the SCID, but did not meet criteria for any other Axis I and II disorders. K. reported mild to moderate symptoms in each of the three DSM-III-R symptom cluster areas for PTSD (American Psychiatric Association, 1987). Her reexperiencing symptoms included nightmares and intrusive daytime recollections, which she referred to as "daymares," and which would often bring her to tears. She had frequent intrusive fantasies of catastrophic events as she went about her daily life (e.g., buildings falling on people on the street). K.'s avoidant symptoms included avoiding thoughts about the attack, avoiding reminders of it (e.g., the area around the World Trade Center), and avoiding situations where she perceived herself to be especially vulnerable (e.g., riding the subway). Although usually outgoing and socially engaged, K. was also aware of feeling "distant or cut off" from others. K. was raised in a Catholic family in a working class neighborhood and reportedly enjoyed a close relationship with her family, her boyfriend and many friends, but had felt removed from those relationships since the bombing despite their offers of support. Her symptoms of hyperarousal included difficulty sleeping and concentrating, as well as an exaggerated startle response. She noted that her difficulty falling asleep preceded the bombing, but had become worse since then. K. was especially disturbed by her impaired concentration, particularly at work. She denied feeling irritable, but the examiner suspected that she minimized this aspect of her experience.

In closing the interview, K., with pride, described her independence and self-efficacy at work and in her social relationships. She noted that it was difficult for her to acknowledge, for perhaps the first time in her adult life, she could not solve her problems and needed psychotherapy. She had never received psychiatric treatment prior to the WTC bombing.

TREATMENT

Cognitive Processing Therapy

The treatment was adapted from Cognitive Processing Therapy (CPT) (Resick & Schnicke, 1992; 1993) and was supervised by one of the authors (J.D.), who had previously been trained in the use of CPT by Resick's research group. K. learned a cognitive model of PTSD. She was taught to identify maladaptive cognitions that develop following trauma, to link these cognitions to her affect and PTSD symptoms, and to challenge her maladaptive thoughts (Beck & Emery, 1985). The treatment, thus, emphasized cognitive restructuring. The exposure component of the treatment consisted of having K. on two occasions write in detail about her experience of the bombing. She read and reviewed those writings in session, as with all of the homework assignments. The treatment also systematically addressed five areas hypothesized to be affected by trauma: safety, trust, power, esteem, and intimacy (McCann, Sakheim, & Abrahamson, 1988). Based on the CPT manual, each session had a goal and a homework assignment. Typically, K. was asked to write about her experience (e.g., to recall the trauma or to reflect on the meaning of the event), and to review the homework in session. K. was seen for 12, 50 minute individual psychotherapy sessions. (The content of each of the sessions is summarized in Table 1.)

Course of Treatment

Although K. was referred for treatment during her initial evaluation, she postponed it to address the rehabilitation of her arm. When she started psychotherapy, she was still spending about 20 hours per week undergoing physical therapy. By the time K. began treatment four months after her initial evaluation, she believed that she had improved significantly

TABLE 1. Summary of Treatment Sessions

Session Number	Content
1	Information gathering; presentation of information processing model of PTSD
2	Review written homework on the meaning of the event; introduction of the idea of "stuck points"; education regarding the link between thoughts and feelings
3	Review A-B-C homework sheets
4-5	Read and discuss written account of the explosion; identification of "stuck points"
6-7	Identification of maladaptive beliefs and thought patterns; review of challenging beliefs worksheets
7-11	Introduction of five themes: safety, trust, power, esteem, & intimacy
12	Review of second written account of the meaning of the event; review of treatment; discussion of future plans

and that she was functioning at about 60% of her pretrauma capacity. She had not returned to work, however. Her initial presentation in therapy suggested that she overestimated the extent of both her physical and psychological recovery. K.'s self-reported improvement was consistent with her tendency to minimize her difficulties.

K. stated that her sense of herself was "completely shaken" by the bombing, but in a manner that offered her the chance to make changes in her life. She was an active participant in the therapy who quickly learned to identify and challenge her maladaptive cognitions. Three broad themes emerged during treatment. She described feeling that it was unfair that her life was disrupted by the bombing. K. discussed her realization that there was more evil in the world than she had previously thought. She believed that her Catholic upbringing had shaped her beliefs about the world, noting that she was taught to abide by the "golden rule" of do unto others as you would have them do unto you. However, the bombing led her to realize that many people did not share this belief. She found this realization very disturbing. K. also focused on how the bombing led her to confront her mortality.

During the course of treatment, K. decided that she wanted to change the priorities in her life; up to the time of the bombing K. had devoted most of her life to her career, and had been very successful. As her treatment progressed, she decided that she wanted to emphasize relationships more and her career less. She also wanted to start a family. K. made what she described as two very important decisions: She did not return to her previous job and she began to search for a new one. K also broke up with her boyfriend. By the end of treatment, according to her self-report and as indicated by her scores on the assessment measures, K. was nearly free of PTSD symptoms (see Table 2).

Follow-Up

One year. At the one-year follow-up, during her first trip back to the New York metropolitan area, K. reported that she was doing well and that psychotherapy had helped her to understand her PTSD symptoms and reorder her life priorities. She had taken a job in a new city, which she liked, and had developed a relationship with a man whom she later married. Though she no longer met criteria for PTSD on the SCID, her self-report scores on the symptoms measures were higher than the initial pretreatment, scores, and much higher than her end of treatment scores.

Two and a half years. The two and half year follow-up interview was conducted by phone by the other author (D.E.). Based on the Clinician Administered PTSD Scale (CAPS) (Blake, Weathers, Nagy et al., 1992), K. did not meet the DSM-IV criteria for PTSD; nor did she report symptoms consistent with any other psychiatric diagnosis. She did report, however, on-going difficulties with concentration, memory, and sleep, albeit minor ones. She did not feel that these difficulties significantly interfered with her work performance, or with other areas of her life, but she felt that she was not quite as "sharp" as she once had been. However, she noted that she still managed her household effectively and was sharper than the great majority of people with whom she worked.

K.'s responses to the self-report measures from this follow-up showed a drop in PTSD symptoms to levels similar to, but slightly lower, than when treatment ended; for example, her total score on the PSS changed from 11 at the start of treatment, indicating "moderate" PTSD, (Nishith, Hearst, Muesser, & Foa, 1995) to 3, indicating "no" or "mild" PTSD at the end of treatment, to 19 ("moderate") at the one year follow-up and to 2 ("no" or "mild") at the two and a half year follow-up (see Table 2).

When asked to reflect on the impact of the bombing on her life, K. stated that on the whole the bombing had opened a door to very positive changes in her life. She described the bombing as a "wake up call." K. commented on a sense of irony about having benefited from such a destructive event, saying "unfortunately, it was good for me." She reported that her life was much better now and more "balanced," than it had been prior to the bombing. K. recalled how the spring after her treatment she went on a long trip that allowed her to spend a significant amount of time

TABLE 2. Scores of Self-Report Assessment Measures

Session/Follow-Up	S1	S6	S10	S11	S12	1 yr	2.5 yrs
PTSD Sx Total	11	8	11	9	3	19	2
(a) Reexperiencing	2	1	1	3	1	5	0
(b) Avoidance	5	0	1	0	0	7	0
(c) Arousal	4	7	9	6	2	7	2
BSI-GSI	.49	.25	.30	.19	.11	.66	.25
Depression	.57	00	.43	.14	.14	.86	00
Anxiety	.50	.17	.17	00	00	.67	0

in the outdoors engaged in vigorous activity (e.g., hiking) for the first time since her injury; she noted that on this trip she was aware of loving the feeling of being alive. She said that this sense of having a new appreciation for her life has been sustained. K. stated since the bombing and subsequent treatment she discovered much of what felt lacking in her life prior to the bombing. She had married and was pregnant at the time of the interview. She added that she was preparing to move back to the New York area to be closer to her family in anticipation of the birth of her first child. She acknowledged that her treatment was an important part of making those changes.

DISCUSSION

The present case describes the successful adaptation of Cognitive Processing Therapy (Resick & Schnicke, 1992; 1993), originally developed for the treatment of PTSD and depression in survivors of sexual assault, for the treatment of PTSD following a terrorist incident. No major modifications of the manual were required to address the PTSD symptoms. The relative ease with which CPT was adapted to the present case supports the observation that while the content of PTSD symptoms are likely to vary with different traumas, the structure of the symptoms may be similar and may respond to similar treatments. K.'s case also affirms the importance of focusing on the impact of the trauma on the patient's view of the world and of herself in addition to the direct PTSD symptomatology (Janoff-Bulman, 1989).

The cognitive model on which CPT is based emphasizes the importance of how beliefs about the self, others, and the world are altered by trauma. In contrast to behavioral models (e.g., Keane, Zimmerling, &

Cadell, 1985) of PTSD which explain PTSD as a generalization of conditioned response, both psychodynamic (Horowitz, 1986) and cognitive models of PTSD (Foa, Steketee, & Rothbaum, 1989; Janoff-Bulman, 1989) have focused on the meaning of the trauma and on the need to reorganize beliefs about the world in order to accommodate the experience of the traumatic event. Resick and Schnicke's (1992) treatment focuses on aiding the integration of the traumatic experience into schemas about the self and the world in an adaptive manner. Building upon the work of Hollon and Garber (1988), Resick and Schnicke (1992) argue that PTSD may be associated with two types of maladaptive cognition: (1) assimilation of the event into existing beliefs, but in a manner which alters information about the experience; and (2) over-accommodating, which refers to changing one's beliefs about the world to accommodate to the information provided by the event, but in a manner which gives the event too much priority in determining one's beliefs about the world.

In arguing for a model of PTSD which addresses the meaning of the trauma, Foa and her colleagues (1989) note research (Scheppele & Bart, 1983) which shows that women who are raped are more likely to develop PTSD if the rape occurs in a familiar place and/or by a familiar person. They also point to research (Sales, Baum, & Shore, 1984; Kilpatrick, Best, Veronen, Villeponteaux, & Amick-McMullen, 1986), which indicates the importance of the threat *perceived* by the victim in the development of PTSD. Traumatic events which challenge strongly held and important beliefs, e.g., "I am safe at work," or "People are motivated more by good than by evil," may be more likely to lead to the development of PTSD symptoms. For K. the beliefs that she was safe going about her business in places known to her and that people generally were good were undermined by the WTC bombing, leaving her feeling vulnerable and confused. K. had also believed in her own efficacy, but the WTC bombing and her physical and mental state following the bombing, left her doubting her abilities.

In Resick and Schnicke's model, K. might be described as "over-accommodating" in as much as she came to see "evil as equal in power in the world as good" and expected traumatic events to occur routinely, whenever she walked down the street. She went from expecting the world to be benign and experiencing herself as highly successful and in charge of her life, to thinking that evil and danger were constant threats and that she was incapable of doing her job. K. can also be described as altering information about the event. For example, she denied the extent of her physical and psychological disability following the bombing and joked about her own brush with death.

Treatment was helpful in challenging the probability of occurrence of the catastrophes she imagined, while still recognizing that tragedies do occur. In the process, K. began to integrate the trauma into a more adaptive conceptualization of the world.

Treatment also helped her to acknowledge how much her life had been disrupted by the bombing and her injuries and helped her to process her emotional response to it. Emotional processing was facilitated by providing exposure to the memory of the event and encouraging her to experience her emotions instead of avoiding memories of the bombing. The treatment also helped K. to sort out her priorities in life. The last five sessions, which focused on five specific life areas, safety, trust, power, esteem, and intimacy, hypothesized to be affected by trauma, were broad enough in scope to help her address her present concerns and her desire to make changes in her life. She began to make decisions about her career and her relationships in light of her evolving conceptualization of the world and of herself. K. noted that simply having the PTSD diagnosis and understanding the cognitive model of PTSD helped her to feel less confused.

K.'s case also demonstrates the potential for an adaptive response to traumatic events facilitated by psychotherapy. While her symptoms of PTSD were distressing and problematic for her, in facing the trauma and its ramifications, she reported that she was able to reorganize her priorities and to make significant changes. The trauma forced her to reconsider decisions she had made about her life, and so became an opportunity. This description of K.'s coming to terms with the WTC bombing is reminiscent of existential philosophers and psychotherapists (e.g., Yalom, 1980), who, like cognitive theorists, also emphasize the primacy of meaning in psychological life. Yalom (1980) writes of how the awareness of death often casts important decisions in a new light. K. stated that her confrontation with death had helped her to reorient her priorities in life. K. expressed the concern in an early session that the therapist wanted to focus on the bombing, while she was more concerned about her future. K. and the therapist were able to address this concern, in part, by linking her existential concerns about the future and about her mortality to the trauma and her subsequent PTSD symptoms. While her focus on the future may have been partly an attempt to avoid the distress of recalling how frightening the bombing had been, it also reflected a new experience of herself, the world, and others.

This case also highlights the variable course of PTSD symptoms, even in a successful treatment. While both self-report measures showed a general decline over the course of treatment to very low levels at the end of treatment, at the one year follow-up most of the measures were higher than at the start of treatment. A year and a half later, however, the scores of all the measures had returned to very low levels, similar to the end of treatment.

Two possible explanations help to make sense of the increase in symptoms at the one year follow-up. The first was offered by K. who noted that when she was in treatment she thought frequently about the bombing; her symptoms were also frequent and often intense. At follow-up, the occurrence of symptoms was more jarring for her, because, in contrast, the rest of her life was now more settled than during treatment. Thus, her symptoms stood out more in her stream of awareness and so she rated them more strongly. For example, she recalled intense feelings at the time of the first follow-up, in response to viewing a movie of a terrorist attack. The second possibility, which does not exclude the first, is that her first return to the New York area, which coincided with the initial follow-up, led to a re-emergence of her symptoms. Anticipating being in the area where the bombing occurred and then being exposed to sensory cues related to the bombing could have brought on a renewal of symptoms ultimately leading, perhaps, to a more complete integration of the experience.

Regardless of the reasons for the fluctuating course, case studies such as this should give researchers pause when interpreting follow-up data, especially if it is short-term. While randomized studies with control groups are imperative, the present case offers a hopeful account of treating PTSD with current models, regardless of the type of trauma involved. The present case also adds anecdotal evidence to the efficacy of treatment models, which recognize the importance of the meaning of the trauma, and the usefulness of exposure and cognitive techniques in the treatment of PTSD.

REFERENCES

American Psychiatric Association (1987). *Diagnostic and statistical manual of mental disorders* (3rd ed., rev). Washington, D.C.: Author.

Beck, A. T., & Emery, G. (1985). *Anxiety disorders and phobias: A cognitive perspective.* New York, Basic Books.

Blake, D. D., Weathers F., Nagy, L. M., Kaloupek, D., Klauminzer, G., Charney, D., & Keane, T. M. (1990). A clinician rating scale for assessing current and lifetime PTSD: The CAPS. *The Behavior Therapist, 18*, 187-188.

Derogatis, L. R., & Melisaratos, N. (1983). The Brief Symptoms Inventory: An introductory report. *Psychological Medicine, 13*, 595-605.

Difede, J., Apfeldorf, W., Cloitre, M., Speilman, L., & Perry, S. (1997). Acute psychiatric responses to the explosion at the World Trade Center: A case series. *Journal of Nervous and Mental Disease, 186*(1): 3-5.

Foa, E. B., Riggs, D. S., Dancu, C. V., & Rothbaum, B. O. (1993). Reliability and validity of a brief instrument for assessing post-traumatic stress disorder. *Journal of Traumatic Stress, 6*, 459-473.

Foa, E. B., Stekee, G., & Rothbaum, B. (1989). Behavioral/cognitive conceptualization of posttraumatic stress disorder. *Behavior Therapy, 20,* 155-176.

Hollon, S. D., & Garber, J. (1988). Cognitive therapy. In L. Y. Abramson (Ed.), *Social cognition and clinical psychology: A synthesis* (pp. 204-253). New York: Guilford Press.

Horowitz, M. J. (1986). Stress-response syndromes: A review of posttraumatic and adjustment disorders. *Hospital Community Psychiatry, 37*(3), 241-248.

Horowitz, M. J., Wilner, N., & Alvarez, W. (1979). Impact of Events Scale: A measure of subjective distress. *Psychosomatic Medicine, 41*, 209-218.

Janoff-Bulman, R. (1989). Assumptive worlds and the stress of traumatic events: Applications of the schema construct. *Social Cognition, 7*, 113 -13 6.

Keane, T. M., Zimmerling, R. T., & Caddell, J. M. (1985). A behavioral formulation of posttraumatic stress disorder in Vietnam veterans. *The Behavior Therapist, 8*, 9-12.

Kilpatrick, D. G., Best, C. L., Veronen, L. J., Villeponteaux, & Amick-McMullan, A. E. (1986). *Predicting the impact of a stressful life experience: Criminal victimization.* Presented at the seventh annual meeting of the Society of Behavioral Medicine, San Francisco.

McCann, I. L., Sakheim, D. K., & Abrahamson, D. J. (1988). Trauma and victimization: A model of psychological adaptation. *Counseling Psychologist, 16*, 531-594.

Resick, P. A., & Schnicke, M. K. (1992a). Cognitive processing therapy for sexual assault victims. *Journal of Consulting and Clinical Psychology, 60*, 748-756.

Resick, P. A., & Schnicke, M. K. (1993). *Cognitive processing therapy for sexual assault: A treatment manual.* American Psychological Association Press.

Sales, E., Baum, M., & Shore, B. (1984). Victim readjustment following assault. *Journal of Social Issues, 40,* 117-136.

Shalev, A., Bonne, O., & Eth, S. (1996). Treatment of posttraumatic stress disorder: A review. *Psychosomatic Medicine, 58*, 165-182.

Scheppele, K. L., & Bart, P. B. (1983). Through women's eyes: Defining danger in the wake of sexual assault. *Journal of Social Issues, 39*, 63-81.

Solomon, S. D., Gerrity, E. T., & Muff, A. M. (1992). Efficacy of treatments for posttraumatic stress disorder. *Journal of the American Medical Association, 268*, 633-638.

Spitzer, R. L., Williams, J. B. W., & Gibbons, M. (1987). *Structured clinical interview for DSM-III-R (SCID).* New York: Biometrics Research Department, New York State Psychiatric Institute.

Yalom, I. (1980). *Existential psychotherapy.* New York: Basic Books.

Index

